CULTS
THAT KILL

CULTS THAT KILL

Shocking True Stories of Horror of
**Psychopathic Leaders, Doomsday Prophets,
Brainwashed Followers, Human Sacrifices,
Mass Suicides and Grisly Murders**

Wendy Joan Biddlecombe Agsar

Ulysses Press

Published in the United States by:
ULYSSES PRESS
P.O. Box 3440
Berkeley, CA 94703
www.ulyssespress.com

ISBN: 978-1-61243-865-8
Library of Congress Control Number: 2018957016

Printed in Canada by Marquis Book Printing
10 9 8 7 6 5 4 3 2 1

Acquisitions editor: Casie Vogel
Managing editor: Claire Chun
Editor: Renee Rutledge
Proofreader: Shayna Keyles
Front cover design and interior: what!design @ whatweb.com
Cover photo: © Sergey Kamshylin/shutterstock.com

Distributed by Publishers Group West

For Sam

CONTENTS

INTRODUCTION

This is a revolutionary suicide. It's not a self-destructive suicide, so they'll pay for this. They've brought this upon us and they'll pay for that. I leave that destiny to them.

—Jim Jones "Death Tape" transcript from
November 18, 1978

The grizzly photos of 913 departed souls at Jonestown are hard to erase from your memory—rows upon rows of dead men, women, and children splayed out facedown in the mud, or their lifeless eyes gazing into the sky above the jungles of Guyana in South America, where Peoples Temple cult leader Jim Jones had promised them a truly equal society that they would build from the ground up. In reality, his followers had worked long and grueling hours in extreme heat clearing the thick terrain for the settlement. They subsisted on little more than rice and beans and were constantly subjected to Jones's paranoia, delusions, and violence in the form of 24-hour sermons broadcast over loudspeakers that could be heard all throughout Jonestown; loyalty tests that encouraged members to inform on anyone who expressed a desire to leave; mock-suicide drills; and sexual abuse.

In November 1978, a delegation led by California Congressman Leo Ryan showed up to check on the welfare of Jonestown residents, many of whom had concerned family members back in the US who believed Jones was holding their mothers, brothers, and cousins against their will. The visit went smoothly at first, with a tour of the compound and evening entertainment performed for Ryan and his crew, but the following day, chaos ensued when Peoples Temple members told Ryan and his entourage that they wanted to defect and leave with him on the next flight out. Ryan and his group made it as far as a nearby airport before they were ambushed. Ryan and three other people died on the airstrip, while 10 others were wounded and waited nearly 24 hours before being rescued and receiving medical attention.

Back at Jonestown, Jones told his members that it was all over, that he'd had a prophecy that a man on Ryan's plane would shoot the pilot in the head and the people of Jonestown would be blamed, their children tortured. There was no other choice, Jones said, but to end it all. Jones urged his followers to ingest a deadly combination of Flavor Aid and cyanide, and a fleet of armed guards ensured his wishes were carried out. Parents squirted the deadly poison down their children's throats and watched them foam at the mouth; elderly residents were forcibly injected. Other people were shot, as well as the dogs and cats that lived in the commune, and within hours Jonestown became the largest mass suicide in modern history (though survivors claim it was murder, not suicide, that claimed all those lives).

Flash forward nearly 20 years to the iconic and chilling photos of the 39 members of Heaven's Gate lying lifeless in bunk beds, shrouded in purple sheets, and wearing black Nike Decades and armbands reading "Heaven's Gate Away Team." The UFO cult members, many of whom worked as computer programmers and web developers, believed that the appearance of the Hale-Bopp comet near Earth was the opportunity they'd been waiting for to get transported to the next "human evolutionary level." Under the leadership of Marshall Applewhite, the cult members drank vodka and ate a mix of applesauce or pudding cut with phenobarbital (an anti-seizure medication), and tied a plastic bag around each others' heads to speed up the process.

Killing yourself so you can be united with aliens in outer space? Giving your own child cyanide to drink? *No way*, you're likely thinking. *I would never do that.* It's hard to imagine being swept up by Jones, Applewhite, or another charismatic cult leader to the point where you'd do anything they said and follow any order they gave, including murder or another bizarre criminal act. But these photos are proof that regular, everyday people have and continue to join cults, which often promote a very different message than the one they use to lure people to join.

Thousands of cults around the world are active today, and it's estimated that between 2 and 5 million Americans have been involved in a cult at some point in their life. Certainly not all cults commit murder or force their members into mass suicide. And it's true that only the most extreme, gruesome, and nefarious cults ever make it into the news. But many cults do share similar characteristics, such as an unwavering faith in an absolute leader and an intense devotion to an ideological cause, that lays the groundwork and possibility for criminal acts to take place—especially when the leader is backed into a corner, as Jones was with a congressman and news team infiltrating his utopian commune.

Looking back at the disturbing photos from Jonestown or grainy television footage of the Heaven's Gate mansion, one might think these were bizarre acts of a far-off, low-resolution, bygone age. But we still live with the aftershocks of these cults today, in addition to new cult activity, and continue to be fascinated by every new twist and turn in these sagas. Here are just a few examples:

♣ When Charles Manson died on November 19, 2017, his body sat on ice in a top-secret location for four months as four men stepped forward to stake their claim to the maniacal mastermind's body.

♣ The following spring, the Netflix documentary *Wild Wild Country* introduced viewers to the Indian spiritual leader Bhagwan Shree Rajneesh and the unthinkable actions of his followers to take over and maintain political control of the small town of Antelope, Oregon, in the 1980s, where they orchestrated a mass salmonella poisoning.

♣ Twenty-three years after the 1995 sarin chemical attack in the Tokyo subway that killed 13 people and sickened thousands of others, Japan executed 13 members of Aum Shinrikyo in two waves in July 2018. This doomsday cult, which recruited new members at prestigious universities, was led by Shoko Asahara, who believed that he was both Jesus Christ and the first enlightened person since the Buddha.

♣ In late 2018, a sex trafficking case continued to be built against Keith Raniere, who founded a multilevel marketing company called NXIVM in the 1990s. The organization has since taught an estimated 16,000 people how to "raise human awareness, foster an ethical humanitarian civilization, and celebrate what it means to be human," according to their website. The courses, which detractors allege use mind-control techniques, cost thousands of dollars to join. In the fall of 2017, several women told the *New York Times* reporter Barry Meier that NXIVM, had a secret inner group call DOS, where women were branded with a cauterizing instrument below their hip during initiation and blackmailed into becoming sex slaves. After the *Times* story, as well as a civilian investigation by a high-profile former member, Rainere was arrested along with others in the organization, including actress Allison Mack and Seagram liquor heiress Clare Bronfman.

In *Cults That Kill*, you'll learn more about the biggest cult murders of the twentieth century, including Jonestown, Heaven's Gate, and the Manson Family killings—which ended the so-called "Summer of Love" and spread fear through Los Angeles and beyond for the senseless and brutal acts. You'll also learn about lesser-known but equally horrifying cults, including a Canadian commune where a cult leader who went by the moniker "Moses" performed horrific medical procedures on his many wives and other followers, a teenage vampire who bludgeoned a Florida couple to death, an elite cult modeled after the Knights Templar that encouraged hundreds of their followers to commit ritual suicide, and a small family cult in Mexico that sacrificed two boys and an older woman to "Saint Death" in this millennium.

Along the way, you'll learn more about the psychology behind cult figureheads, learn about what kinds of people are most susceptible to cult indoctrination, find out the difference between a cult and a legitimate religious offshoot, and discover the similarities among these charismatic leaders who can control or convince their followers to do just about anything (even murder).

CHAPTER 1

WHAT IS A CULT?

Cults are defined as groups of people who have joined together for an ideological cause, such as religion, politics, science fiction, or self-improvement, and are under the total control of a charismatic leader to whom they are completely devoted. Cult beliefs are all-consuming, and cults usually isolate themselves, shunning the outside world to prevent conflicting viewpoints, including from the news and media, to permeate the tight-knit group. The cult leader, who can be alive or dead, is always right, has important information that only they know (such as the day the world will end or biblical secrets), and cannot be questioned by his or her followers.

You don't look for cults; cults look for you. And people don't knowingly join cults, but instead join religious, political, or self-improvement organizations with a mission that resonates with them. Cults have specific tactics for recruiting new members, and people who are lonely, vulnerable, or going through major life changes are often targeted. Some reported tactics include sending cult members to university registrar offices to befriend someone who has dropped a class or to stake out potential new members leaving school counseling centers. Another way that cults recruit is through legitimate businesses. An apocalyptic Christian cult called the Twelve Tribes, which has been accused of child abuse and anti-Semitism, runs cafes all over the world that, according to a *Vice* headline, serves food that is "so good you forget it's run by a cult." Church functions, yoga, and meditation classes are also a prime location for recruiters to pounce on people who appear lonely and vulnerable. Once an initial contact is made, cults often shower a potential recruit with love, friendship, and acceptance to make their group appealing and to start the process of brainwashing or other forms of psychological control.

Dr. Janja Lalich, professor emerita of sociology at California State University, Chico, and a former member of a now-defunct cult called the Democratic Workers Party, says that even in today's digital age, cults continue to rely on personal contact to seal the deal, and an estimated two-thirds of cult members are introduced to the organization through a family member.

Once a potential member has been identified, a swift indoctrination process starts, which can include long meetings with the group, sleep deprivation, isolation, and control of daily activities. These tactics, many of which are brainwashing or mind-control tools, chip away at an individual's critical thinking skills to the point where group-think moves into the forefront of one's thoughts.

Ian Haworth, director of the United Kingdom's Cult Information Centre, has said that his introduction to PSI Mind Development

Institute happened when he was approached in Toronto and asked to fill out a survey. PSI was a large group-awareness training program that promised to teach him how to excel at personal and professional relationships through better communication, confidence, as well as increased creativity and productivity. Haworth's introduction to the group quickly led to him taking a four-day course on quitting smoking, after which Haworth resigned from his well-paying business job and gave all his money to the organization.

A common misperception is that only unintelligent and easily impressionable people can be stupid enough to be swept up by a cult. In *The Changing Face of Terrorism*, scholar Benjamin Cole explains that the opposite is usually true. "Healthy minds that are intellectually alert and inquisitive, and perhaps idealistic, are in fact the easiest to recruit and control," Cole writes. Haworth has echoed this, calling the idea that "troubled people" join a cult an "eternal myth." It is the "strong-willed, strong-minded person" who is quickly broken down, Haworth said in a *Vice* interview.

Dr. Margaret Singer, the late preeminent cult researcher/scholar who began her career studying brainwashing of Korean War prisoners, has said that many recruits are "normal" people who may be lonely and searching for answers. Before she died in 2003, Singer served as an expert witness in many court cases, including the trial of kidnapped media heiress turned guerrilla fighter Patty Hearst, and personally interviewed more than 4,000 cult members.

"Most of them don't recruit in the poor end of town, because people in the poor end are street smart and know when someone's out to steal their lunch money," Singer told *SF Gate* in 2002. A significant exception is Jim Jones's People Temple, which actively recruited in black churches and in the inner cities with promises of an equal society (with Jones eventually taking entire social security checks and other assets).

Cult researcher Steven Hassan, a mental health counselor and former "Moonie"—a follower of cult leader Reverend Sun Myung Moon, who taught his followers that he had been chosen as Jesus's successor and was known for performing mass weddings—has said that vulnerable people not familiar with cult tactics (those who aren't good consumers) are at-risk for cult indoctrination. Much like the misperception that unintelligent people fall prey to cults, the idea that only college-age students join cults is a myth as well. Lalich, who runs the Cult Research and Information Center in addition to pursuing her academic work, has said that she gets more calls from concerned spouses or children worried about their parents, and that people in their thrities and forties with money to contribute to a cult are more desirable for recruiters than a free-spirited dropout.

"I think a lot of the groups have gotten more savvy in the sense of creating front groups and having that as a way people can either recruit or donate money. People might be donating money to something that sounds really wonderful ... but it's going to a cult in the background," Lalich said of cults becoming more sophisticated over time.

Lalich has written that cults haven't disappeared off the face of the earth, but are "thriving," with many cults having "matured" and "claim[ing] to have discontinued some of their more questionable behaviors." In recent years, cults have latched on to preexisting cultural ideologies, such as preserving gun ownership in America, that have a wider appeal in mainstream society than the apocalyptic messages that were so prevalent in past cults.

WHAT MAKES A CULT LEADER?

To gain followers, cult leaders need to have enough clout and persuasion to convince members to leave their old lives behind and join their cause. In *Cults in Our Midst*, Singer and Lalich identify the three characteristics of cult leaders:

> *Cult leaders are self-appointed, persuasive persons who claim to have a special mission in life or to have special knowledge.*
>
> *Cult leaders tend to be determined and domineering, and are often described as charismatic.*
>
> *Cult leaders center veneration on themselves.*

On the surface, cult leaders express a goal of living in a better world—think of Jim Jones's utopian society (more on this on page 53)—but these figures are in actuality driven by a desire for money, sex, power, or a combination of those three things. Cult leaders tend to be men, though not always. Women leaders, such as Bonnie Lu Nettles who cofounded Heaven's Gate, and Lois Roden, who groomed David Koresh to lead the Branch Davidians, have enjoyed a good deal of success at the helm.

Singer and Lalich also maintain that every time there is a great change in society, cult leaders will be waiting in the wings to prey on the vulnerable and find new recruits. In *Cults in Our Midst*, they explain that the major societal changes in the United States in the 1960s—the Vietnam War and counterculture attitude and protests—provided a ripe breeding ground for spiritual cults with roots in the East. In the 1970s, cult trends turned toward Christianity, psychology, and politics for "mind-expanding experiences"; in the 1980s, due to an economic downtick, cults centering around financial prosperity cropped up. Modern cults, not surprisingly given the NXIVM news, often center around self-improvement.

In an interview for this book, Lalich said that business improvement and leadership seminars are "so embedded in our society" that many people often don't know that Large Group Awareness Trainings (LGAT) might have cult ties. Lalich said she worked on a cult case where an entire company had sent their employees to LGAT trainings.

"Then they kind of turned their whole business into a model of the training program by using the same languages, techniques, ostracizing people, and having very emotional sharing in the workplace, which is inappropriate," Lalich said.

TURNING DESTRUCTIVE

In this book, you'll learn more about destructive cults that have different kinds of allegiances, including to Christianity and Eastern religions, as well as with spiritual, racial, and occult ties.

If and when a cult turns toward destruction often depends on the moral compass and aspirations of the cult leader. Lalich has explained that the possibility of destruction is possible when you have an isolated group with a powerful leader. If that leader has any kind of destructive or self-destructive tendencies and is backed into a corner, then destructive acts such as suicides can take place.

According to psychologist Robert Jay Lifton, apocalyptic impulses are actually a part of human nature. "Individual death, when associated with the death and rebirth of the world, can take on special significance and high nobility," Lifton writes, and participating in an "apocalyptic project" offers cult members an opportunity to be part of something larger and eternal.

Steven Hassan has described the "incredible pressure" for members of Peoples Temple, Order of the Solar Temple, and Heaven's Gate to commit mass suicide. "Once they [Heaven's Gate] made those videos and said goodbye to everybody on TV, what were they going to do? Stand up and say 'oh guess what gang, I don't want to do it?'"

CULT VERSUS SECT

There has been some debate as to whether all new religions start out as cults. The *Oxford English Dictionary* defines a cult as a "system of religious veneration and devotion directed toward a particular figure or object." A secondary definition calls a cult a "relatively small group of people having religious beliefs or practices regarded by others as strange or as imposing excessive control over members." A sect, however, is defined as a "group of people with somewhat different religious beliefs (typically regarded as heretical) from those of a larger group to which they belong."

Offshoots of mainstream religious movements—even the Catholic Church—might be called a "cult." The world "cult" took on a more pejorative meaning in the 1970s when it was applied to groups such as the Manson Family or the Children of God, a cult that followed founder David Berg's interpretations of Christianity and in the past promoted sex between adults and children. Dr. Lalich differentiates the two in "Sect or Cult: What's Going Down in Texas?", saying that "in a healthy or legitimate religion or sect, you are presumably worshipping a higher principle or some higher authority ... whereas in a cult people tend to end up worshipping that living human leader."

In Chapter 10, we'll go over a current saint's cult called Santa Muerte, which blends Catholicism and indigenous Mexican religious beliefs, that has rapidly grown to an estimated 12 million members in 15 years.

LEGAL PROTECTION FOR CULTS

In the United States, many cults are registered religious organizations, some receiving nonprofit charity status, and enjoy freedom of religion under the First Amendment. Because of this distinction, it is hard for courts to take legal action against questionable groups if they are not committing crimes.

In Chapter 6, you'll learn how the French legislature responded to a ritual killing by a group called the Solar Temple, and the laws they introduced to closely monitor cults that are active in their country.

The US did, however, see several lawsuits related to "deprogramming," a tactic that emerged from the US cult hysteria. Concerned family members hired a deprogrammer to essentially abduct the alleged cult member and hold them indefinitely until their family could convince them to return home. The "father of deprogramming" is a California man named Ted Patrick who made the controversial practice his profession after his son was swept up in the Children of God. Patrick had no formal training as a mental health expert and was sued and jailed multiple times on kidnapping charges. Due to the legal pressures, many "experts" stopped practicing deprogramming in the 1990s.

CHAPTER 2

CHARLES MANSON AND THE MANSON FAMILY

"Evil Dead," "Burn in Hell." These tabloid newspaper headlines did not mince words when they announced the death of Charles Manson in November 2017.

Manson was a real-life boogeyman, sentenced to life in prison after convincing several of his LSD-fueled followers to tie up and brutally murder nine strangers in 1969. The victims, who included actress Sharon Tate, a coffee heiress, and small business owners, were repeatedly stabbed to death, and Manson's followers, called the Manson Family, wrote cryptic messages such as "Pig" and "Helter Skelter" with their victims' blood.

Perhaps even more shocking than the fact that a small, crazy-eyed man was able to convince multiple men and women to kill for him was who did the killing. They were young "flower children" in their very early twenties who had traveled to California in search of love and finding a new way of being in the world.

The Manson murders, which terrified Los Angeles long after the Manson Family was caught, marked the first known modern instance of destructive cult murders in the United States. Manson provided a dark end to this revolutionary era of assassinations, fights for civil rights, anti-Vietnam war fervor, and a rebellion against conservative values.

"Many people I know in Los Angeles believe that the sixties ended abruptly on August 9, 1969," wrote native Californian, journalist, and novelist Joan Didion. Her sentiment was echoed by Manson trial prosecutor Vincent Bugliosi. Bugliosi has said the reason Manson captivated the word wasn't the "extreme brutality" of the crimes or the celebrity victims, but "the fact that they are the most bizarre murders in the recorded annals of American crime," complete with Bible quotes, Beatles lyrics written in blood, and kids-next-door for killers. "If they had been written as fiction no one would have read it," Bugliosi told the *Guardian* on the fortieth anniversary of the slayings.

EARLY LIFE

Charles Milles Manson was born on November 12, 1934, in Cincinnati, Ohio, to a 16-year-old unmarried mother named Kathleen Maddox. Manson's birth certificate listed him as "No Name Maddox" due to no father being named on the document. Manson claimed he only met his father, a local mill worker, twice. Maddox married William Eugene Manson, who worked at a local dry cleaner, a few months before Charles was born. They divorced three years later.

Manson's childhood was defined by his absent mother and his longing to be taken care of by her. Manson maintains that he was first deserted by his mother for a pitcher of beer.

"Mom was in a cafe one afternoon with me on her lap," Manson and ex-con coauthor Nuel Emmons wrote in *Manson in His Own Words*. "The waitress, a would-be mother without a child of her own, jokingly told my mom she'd buy me from her. Mom replied, 'A pitcher of beer and he's yours.'" Manson's mother downed the pitcher and left her son behind. "Several days later my uncle had to search the town for the waitress and take me home."

Manson's mother made a more permanent disappearance around the time he was six, when she was sent to prison for a robbery she had committed with her brother. Manson spent his childhood with relatives in West Virginia, the closest location to the federal penitentiary at Moundsville, where Maddox was serving her five-year sentence.

According to *The Life and Times of Charles Manson*, the future cult leader was small—closer in size to a toddler than the five-year-olds in his class. From a very young age, he lied, acted out, and insisted on being the center of attention. The first offense that put Manson on the path to becoming a career criminal, according to Manson, started when he was just seven. It was shortly after Christmas, and neighborhood kids were showing off all the presents they had received. Charlie had only gotten one gift that year: a Superman hairbrush that his grandmother told him would make him fly if he brushed his hair with it. Manson said that one day, he rounded up all the neighborhood kids' toys and took them back to his house, where he built a fire and destroyed them.

"Even now, I'm not sure if I just resented being laughed at," Manson recalled in *Manson in His Own Words*. "The kids were mad—some cried, others threatened me, and their parents called the sheriff. And though I wasn't taken to the jail, it was my first encounter with the police."

Manson was briefly reunited with his mother after she was released from federal prison. Manson was a handful—and so was Maddox. Manson's mother landed a job as a grocery store clerk out of prison. She spent her free time drinking and running around with men (sometimes skipping town with them). Manson showed up at her work, hustling customers for pennies to buy candy. In an attempt to get on the straight and narrow, Maddox joined Alcoholics Anonymous and married a man she met at a meeting.

Before the time he was a teenager, Manson was breaking into stores and emptying the cash registers, and stealing guns from family members. He was sent to jail for the first time when he was 12 years old. Manson spent his teenage years in reform schools and juvenile delinquent halls, including the Gibault Home for Boys in Terre Haute, Indiana; Boys Town in Omaha; the Indiana School for Boys; and the National Training School for Boys in Washington, D.C., after Maddox petitioned for her uncontrollable son to become a ward of the state. During his time in these institutions, from which he occasionally tried to escape, Manson claimed that he was physically and sexually abused, witnessed rapes, and was raped himself.

In a paper published by the *International Journal of Offender Therapy and Comparative Criminology*, researchers Andrew J. Atchison and Kathleen M. Heide apply several sociological theories to Manson, his followers, and Manson's childhood and subsequent rise to master manipulator. One of these is labeling theory, the idea that after a primary deviance occurs, an individual embraces the label given to them by society. "Defined as bad, they come to see themselves as bad," Atchison and Heide write. "Consistent with a self-fulfilling prophecy, these individuals then embrace this deviant label by committing more criminal acts, and they become locked into their deviant roles."

Manson was called "trouble" after rounding up toys from the neighborhood and setting them on fire, and a "ringleader" after orchestrating an escape of about 35 other boys who lived in the Indianapolis City Juvenile Home. If society said Charlie was bad, that's what they were going to get—a sentiment that Manson echoed in *Mason in His Own Words*: "If you keep pushing something off on a person, pretty soon that person stops fighting the reputation and becomes everything he is accused of being."

The authors also attribute Manson's criminal escalation to social learning theory, the idea that criminal behavior is learned from others. Manson had plenty of examples as he was shuffled to reform schools across the country. Manson also learned not to trust authority figures early on, since school administrators turned a blind eye to sexual assault and were mentally and physically abusive themselves.

Manson was imprisoned on various offenses committed during his reform school stays, including driving a stolen car across state lines in 1954. In early 1955, when Manson was 20, he met and fell in love with a teenager named Rosalie Jean Willis. They settled down in West Virginia, and Manson fell back on his talents for stealing and transporting cars to make ends meet when Rosalie got pregnant. A boosted Mercury took Manson and his wife all the way to Los Angeles, where he planned to reconnect with his mother. Manson reported that he was having the time of his life on the West Coast but held on to the stolen car as if his name was on the registration. It wasn't, and a serious of court twists and turns connected Manson with several car thefts. He and Rosalie fled to Indiana, where Charles Manson Jr. was born. Manson was taken into custody four days later and extradited back to California the next month. Manson, 21 at this point, had aged out of reform school and was ordered to serve three years at Terminal Island Federal Correctional Institution, a low-security federal prison in the Los Angeles Harbor.

Manson slipped back into life behind bars. Rosalie visited for a year or so, then ran off with a trucker. Manson had a taste of freedom, during which he married a second woman named Leona "Candy" Stevens, but eventually violated his parole with series of soliciting prostitution charges and by trying to cash a fake check. Manson served a portion of his sentence at the McNeil Island federal penitentiary in Washington State, passing the 10 years by learning guitar from Alvin "Creepy" Karpis, reading books on science fiction and Eastern religions, and dabbling in Scientology. In anticipation of his release, Manson was transferred back to Terminal Island in Los Angeles in the summer of 1966, and the following summer, when he was 32 years old, Manson walked out of prison. As the story goes, he asked the guards to stay. Prison was his home, he said. He didn't have anywhere else to go.

THE GARDENER OF HAIGHT-ASHBURY

Just because he didn't have a family to go home to didn't mean that Manson couldn't create one of his own.

Manson found a very different world waiting for him when he got off Terminal Island in 1967. It had been five years since the US upped their presence in Vietnam and two years after the start of Operation Rolling Thunder—a nearly four-year bombing campaign in North Vietnam aimed at getting the North Vietnamese to withdraw their support for the Viet Cong (the opposite happened, as the bombs killed some 182,000 civilians). The military exercise was killing hundreds of US pilots, too, and leaders, including Dr. Martin Luther King Jr., had announced their opposition to the increasingly unpopular war. Teach-ins were organized, and protesters marched to call attention to what they saw as senseless killings. The Civil Rights Movement was well underway and two years earlier, riots in the Watts neighborhood of Los Angeles, protesting police brutality against minorities, had led to 34 deaths.

The summer of Manson's release, young people from all corners of the United States descended on San Francisco, enticed by sex, drugs, rock 'n' roll, and the counterculture idea that there were other ways to exist in this world. The unofficial kick-off was the "Human Be-In" in San Francisco's Golden Gate Park that drew a crowd of 20,000 to protest a recent ban on LSD and more broadly rebel against mainstream values. An estimated 100,000 people descended on the city that summer, wearing bell bottoms and flowers in their long hair, to drop acid and break down the boundaries of society's expectations. That summer "divid[ed] American culture into a Before and After unparalleled since World War II," Sheila Weller, author of *Girls Like Us: Carole King, Joni Mitchell, Carly Simon—and the Journey of a Generation*, wrote in a *Vanity Fair* article. "If you were between 15 and 30 that year, it was almost impossible to resist the lure of the transcendent, peer-driven season of glamour, ecstasy, and Utopianism." Embracing the groundwork laid by the Beat Generation a decade earlier, these "hippies" lived communally in homes in Haight-Ashbury where rent was cheap, or crossed the state in converted vans or school buses, attending music festivals and anti-war protests.

Jay Thelin, a member of the Summer of Love Council who co-owned the Psychedelic Shop on Haight Street, said the movement was about young people not being able to relate to the "activities that the older generation are engaged in."

"Those activities for us are meaningless," Thelin says in a 2017 article in the *New York Times*. "They have led to a monstrous war in Vietnam, for example. And that's why it's all related, the psychedelics and the war and the gap in the generations."

Manson hitchhiked to the Bay Area that summer. With long hair and a guitar, he looked the part and spoke the language.

"All your children were coming to me because no one ever told them the truth," Manson would declare years later.

To appeal to the young people fleeing their nuclear families and conventional paths, Manson relied on a lifetime of crime, his previous career experience as a pimp, and tips of the trade he learned from author and lecturer Dale Carnegie's book *How to Win Friends and Influence People* in a prison self-help class. He was a magnet for many young, middle-class, and upper middle-class men and women who had moved to California in search of another way of living, leaving behind divorced parents and the pressures of conforming to a straight path in traditional society.

Lynette "Squeaky" Fromme, a member of the Family who was imprisoned for attempting to assassinate President Gerald Ford, described him as a "hobo with a touch of class." Southern California native, homecoming princess, and future Manson murderer Leslie Van Houten recalls that in the beginning, being one of "Charlie's girls" was a fun and innocent game, and that Manson filled a void left by her absent father.

"I was desperately seeking someone that I could love and hold on to and call my own," Van Houten recalled of her attraction and devotion to Manson.

Manson primarily preyed upon young women who could help attract male followers, but other men were enticed by Manson without any outside help from the fairer sex. Charles "Tex" Watson grew up in a religious household in Copeville, Texas.

Watson excelled at sports in high school and graduated with honors before heading off to North Texas State University. Watson was lured by the freedom of California and decided to make the permanent move in August 1967.

Watson met Manson after he picked up a hitchhiker, who ended up being Dennis Wilson from The Beach Boys. It was back at Wilson's home that Watson first saw Manson, surrounded by five or six girls, his guitar in his lap. Watson told researchers Atchison and Heide the first thing he noticed in Manson's face was a sort of gentleness, an embracing kind of acceptance and love. Sitting with the group and smoking marijuana, Watson realized that Manson was the first person he met "who really knew what love was all about."

During the summer of love, Manson grew into a role he had created for himself: the "gardener" of Haight-Ashbury, who tended to all the flower children, inviting them to drop their egos. Manson's followers took large amounts of LSD, with Manson taking a smaller dose or abstaining from the hallucinogen outright. Manson also encouraged group sex to break down society's rigid views of sexuality. By summer's end, Manson had about eight full-time followers.

After the summer ended, Manson and his followers traveled south to Los Angeles in an old school bus, dumpster diving or stealing food to eat. They shacked up with Beach Boy Brian Wilson for a spell in his Pacific Palisades home as Manson pursued a music career with a lot of maybes and a few recording sessions, but no signed contracts. According to Curbed Los Angeles, the Manson women did all the household chores, but by the time Wilson's manager kicked Manson and his crew out in August 1968, their stay cost Wilson an estimated $100,000 (which included a visit to a "local sexual health clinic"). The Manson Family eventually put down roots at Spahn Ranch, a 500-acre ranch that started as a homestead and was later turned into a set for Western films. Owner George Spahn was 80 and nearly blind, and allowed the Family to live there for free if they cooked for his crew of rotating cowboys and assisted on his horse farm. (Apparently, in an effort to experience all that life has to offer, Manson's followers relished walking around barefoot in horse excrement.) Spahn was lonely as well, and Manson follower Squeaky Fromme served as his eyes and as a wife stand-in. Though only 30 miles from downtown Los Angeles, Spahn Ranch was isolated, and Manson used this remoteness as an opportunity to cut off his followers from reality and create his own personal kingdom. They were uninhibited "wood nymphs," sharing clothes or wearing nothing at all, frolicking through the woods with flowers in their hair, racing in dune buggies, taking lots and lots of LSD, and engaging in group sex to break down their inhibitions. They also relied on Manson's expertise as a career car thief, stripping down stolen cars on the property for resale.

But, as prosecutor Vincent Bugliosi noted, there weren't any clocks or newspapers at Spahn Ranch, and Manson created what's described by the book *Helter Skelter* as a "tight little society of his own, with its own value system. It was holistic, complete, and totally at odds with the world outside."

In November 1968, the Beatles released their ninth studio album, *The Beatles*, often referred to as "The White Album" for its minimal cover design. Many of the songs were written while the band was in Rishikesh, India, studying Transcendental

Meditation. On side three of the double album was a song called "Helter Skelter." "Helter Skelter" refers to a British term for a tall amusement park slide (though Manson didn't know that at the time). The track features screaming vocals, a fried and almost manic guitar line, and a thumping base.

Paul McCartney's lyrics, "Look out Helter Skelter!," spoke to Manson, and he believed that the song confirmed the ideas he had believed for a while: that an apocalyptic race war was approaching.

Manson's ideology was a dark counterpoint to the open-mindedness that prevailed in the counterculture. His core teaching was that the US was on the cusp of a race war between white and black Americans. This Armageddon was imminent, and the Family planned to hide out in a Death Valley cave to survive the race war. Manson, who believed he was a manifestation of Jesus Christ, predicted that the blacks would annihilate all the whites but would ultimately be incapable of governing this new world. Manson would come in as leader, enslaving all the blacks.

Manson would later define Helter Skelter as "confusion, literally, that lives inside everyone." Susan Atkins, one of Manson's followers who participated in the murders, was a bit clearer in her testimony, describing Helter Skelter as "the last war on the face of the earth. It would be all the wars that have ever been fought, built one on top of the other... You can't conceive of what it would have been like to see every man judge himself and then take it out on every other man all over the face of the earth."

FBI agents who interviewed Manson after the murders believed the notion of Helter Skelter was a way for him to keep a tight grip on his followers.

FROM FREE LOVE TO IN COLD BLOOD

Manson had an assignment for his right-hand man Tex Watson in August 1969: Take a gun, knives, a change of clothes, and some of the girls, and drive out to 10050 Cielo Drive. The secluded home in Benedict Canyon above Beverly Hills was the former home of Terry Melcher, Doris Day's son and a music producer who had passed on the prospect of releasing Manson's music.

Helter Skelter was starting.

"He said to kill everybody in the house as gruesome as I could," Watson would later testify. "I believe he said something about movie stars living there."

And Manson was right. Melcher didn't live in Benedict Canyon anymore. The Hollywood director Roman Polanski and his wife, Sharon Tate, had moved in. Polanski was away in London on the evening of August 8, 1969, and Tate, an actress best known for her performance in *Valley of the Dolls*, who was eight months pregnant, had been hosting a group of her rich hippie friends: Jay Sebring, 35, Tate's former fiancé and a hairdresser credited with reviving an interest in men's hairstyling; Voytek Frykowski, 37, a writer and producer; and Abigail "Gibby" Folger, 26, a coffee heiress and social activist who was Frykowski's girlfriend. Los Angeles was finally cooling off after a three-day heatwave; Frykowski and Folger were staying with the very pregnant Tate until her husband returned home.

The Manson cultists, driven by Linda Kasabian, a pregnant 20-year-old mother of a young baby and the only Family member who had a valid driver's license, arrived at the secluded home at the end of a cul-de-sac in the early morning hours of August 9, 1969. Kasabian recalled feeling excited that Charlie had chosen her for this mission. The first thing they did was cut the telephone line above the high front gate and scale the fence, lit up by Christmas lights, to the 3.3-acre property.

Steven Parent, 18, had just finished drinking a beer with the live-in caretaker and was driving an Ambassador down the driveway, illuminating it with headlights as the cultists walked up. Although the teenager begged not to be hurt, Watson shot Parent four times and turned off the car. Parent's slumped-over body would be found the next day, the clock radio stopped at 12:15 a.m.

With their first kill out of the way, the crew cased the house for open doors and windows. The house was buttoned up for the night, so Watson started slicing a window screen so that he, Susan Atkins, and Patricia Krenwinkel could get inside.

Once they were in, all hell broke loose. Armed with knives, the attackers rounded up the residents, tied them up, and told them they were about to die.

With the attack underway, Tate begged to be spared, if not for her, then for the life of her baby.

Susan Atkins said, "Look, bitch, I have no mercy for you," and advanced with a knife toward the terrified woman, who was clad only in bikini bottoms and a bra. "You're going to die, and you'd better get used to it."

Tate was stabbed 16 times, including in the abdomen, then suspended by a nylon rope thrown over a ceiling beam.

The Manson cultists killed everyone in Tate's house that night, one by one, stabbing and maiming them a collective 102 times, far more than was necessary to get the job done. Sebring died while holding his hands up to his face, as if to protect himself from yet another blow. One of the cultists had thrown a black towel over Sebring's face and tied his neck to the other end of the ligature around Tate's neck.

Back at the car acting as lookout, Kasabian heard constant screams coming from the home. According to her testimony, she ran back to the house to put a stop to the attacks and saw Frykowski stumbling out, his face covered in blood. Frykowski fell to the ground but eventually got back up and into a struggle with Watson, who repeatedly stabbed and hit him over the head, leaving 13 scalp lacerations from the butt of a gun. When police found Frykowski's body the next morning, he was still clutching the grass with his left fingers and cradling his head with his right arm. While Watson was beating Frykowski, Patricia Krenwinkel was chasing after Folger, who had managed to escape through Sharon's bedroom, with a knife. Folger would die under a fir tree out on the lawn, her presumably white nightgown soaked through with blood.

It was apparent from the beginning that money wasn't a motive (though the Manson Family often resorted to petty crimes to keep themselves fed). Valuables weren't taken from the homes or the bodies. Before fleeing the scene and throwing the murder weapons down the hills, the murderers left one last sign. Using Sharon Tate's blood, they scrawled "PIG" on the front door of the secluded mansion.

"I said if you're going to do something, leave something witchy," Manson said years later in a prison interview, referring to the messages left behind in blood. "Do it well ... leave a sign to let the world know you were there."

When she arrived around 8:30 a.m. the next morning, house-keeper Winifred Chapman noticed the cut phone line. Inside the home, she described a scene that the FBI recorded as "macabre" in a memo, and ran to a neighbor's for help. Chapman was so disturbed that she was treated for shock at UCLA Medical Center. Responding officers didn't even bother to check the bodies for pulses, as the silence, battered faces, bullet wounds, and blood-stained clothes indicated there was no chance these victims were alive.

Police wielding shotguns arrested Cielo Drive caretaker William E. Garretson, hauling him down to the station in the pinstriped bell bottoms he had answered the door in. Garretson, a homesick runaway from Ohio with aspirations of learning to act, was at his residence on the grounds during the attack and claimed not to have heard anything. Garretson told detectives that he had been listening to music at a "medium" level that night, and had noticed two peculiarities: the dead phone line, and his door handle tampered with, as though someone had been trying to get in. He was charged with the murders, but released after the results from a polygraph test indicated that he was telling the truth when he said he wasn't involved.

Neighbors heard more than Garretson did, with one recalling the sound of loud claps that could have been gunshots and another a man's screams. A third neighbor said his hunting dogs, who only were disturbed by gunshots, had started barking.

As the morning unfolded, Tate's agent, William Tennant, arrived to identify the actress, still wearing his tennis clothes. He was sobbing as he left the scene, declining to speak with the reporters who had gathered there. Across the pond, Polanski was distraught and making plans to be on the next flight back to LA. Priests, family, and friends spent the day identifying the other four victims. As the coroner took them to the morgue in body bags and animal control officers took two poodles, a dalmatian, a Weimaraner, and a kitten from the home, one officer described the scene as a battlefield.

The inconceivable killings of a beautiful actress and her friends for seemingly no reason injected a new fear into Hollywood's rich and famous. These "ritualistic killings," as the *Los Angeles Times* declared them on their front page, led to homeowners buying guard dogs and hiring off-duty police officers to stand watch. The local security business boomed, with the number of firms tripling after the slayings. Celebrities like Frank Sinatra skipped town. Those who stayed went the extra mile to protect themselves—a Beverly Hills gun store sold 200 guns in just two days, and it took two weeks to get a locksmith appointment.

"It was just a savage crime committed against people who thought they were absolutely safe, and they thought violence was in Vietnam and other places but not here. Not in California, not among the rich," said *New York Times* contributor Janet Maslin.

THE BODY COUNT RISES

The Cielo Drive murders weren't to Manson's liking. Sloppy, he called them after his crew returned to Spahn Ranch. He decided to send out the original crew, plus two more Family members for the second night of Helter Skelter. This time, he'd tag along. Maybe the race war would start if Manson showed them how to do things properly.

Meanwhile, Leno and Rosemary LaBianca had taken a drive in their green 1968 Thunderbird to Lake Isabella, a popular recreation spot about 150 miles north of Los Angeles. Leno LaBianca, 44, owned the local chain of Gateway Markets. Rosemary, 38, who grew up as an orphan in Arizona, was a successful businesswoman who co-owned a boutique and invested in stocks and bonds.

Rosemary's daughter from a previous marriage, Suzanne, drove back to LA with the LaBiancas that night, their pace slowed down by the motorboat hitched to the back of their vehicle. The radio was on, with updates about the Tate home murders the night before. Suzanne recalled that the news "disturbed" her mother, who'd confided that someone had recently been breaking into their house and letting the dogs outside. Suzanne was dropped off in Los Feliz, a neighborhood in central Los Angeles, just east of Hollywood, around 1 a.m. The LaBiancas lived in the same area, and, before going home, stopped at Leno's regular newsstand for the *Herald Examiner* and some small talk about the scene up in Benedict Canyon. They returned home to 3301 Waverly Drive around two o'clock that the morning.

Manson had attended an LSD party next door to the LaBiancas a year earlier and was somewhat familiar with the neighborhood. After spotting Leno asleep on the couch through a window, Manson and his crew entered the house through an unlocked back door. They bound Leno's hands and woke him up at gunpoint.

Manson dipped out before the killings started, and his lawyers have maintained that Leno and Rosemary, who had been collected from the couple's bedroom, were alive when he left Waverly Drive. Manson took Rosemary's wallet—which would later be found in a gas station in a predominately black part of the city—and gave instructions to his followers as to how to kill the couple.

Tex Watson stabbed Leno as Leslie Van Houten restrained Rosemary. Watson stabbed Rosemary first and then handed the knife over to Van Houten, who gave her at least 14 more wounds.

"We started stabbing and cutting up the lady," Van Houten said in court in 1971.

"I knew that people would die, I knew there would be killing. … I stabbed Mrs. LaBianca in the lower back 16 times because Manson wanted everyone to participate," she would recall years later, as reported in "Charles Manson: Journey into Evil."

When the bodies were discovered by family members the following day, Rosemary had been stabbed in the back and buttocks, and a slash on her jaw indicated that she had put up a struggle before she died. Leno had been stabbed 36 times on the front of his body, and the killers had carved "War" into his stomach and stuck him with a two-pronged carving fork. Both LaBiancas had pillowcases, taken from their bed, over their heads, and a lamp cord was wrapped around Rosemary's neck.

The Manson Family left bloody messages around the house—"Rise," "Death to Pigs," and the misspelled "Healter Skelter" on the refrigerator door. Their gruesome calling card would help investigators eventually link the Tate and LaBianca murders.

THE FAMILY BEHIND BARS

The arrests weren't immediate, keeping Los Angeles (and beyond) on edge. And although similarities in the crimes were apparent, it would take months until police connected the two murders.

Manson and 27 others were arrested at Spahn Ranch on charges of auto theft, and Charlie was booked under his name with the added alias, "aka Jesus Christ, God." Other followers, including Tex Watson and Patricia Krenwinkel, fled California following the murders.

A break in the Tate and LaBianca cases came in November, when Susan Atkins couldn't keep her mouth shut about her role. She gossiped to her cell mates at the Sybil Brand Institute, not leaving out the juicy and horrifying details. After her cellies told prosecutors about what they had heard, Atkins cut an immunity deal with prosecutors in exchange for her testimony against Manson and the other murderers. She recounted the events of August 9 and 10 to a grand jury in December 1969. Three months before the trial was set to start, however, Atkins visited Manson in jail, and afterward told the state's lawyers that she had made the whole thing up.

The trial started in June 1970, with Manson, Atkins, Van Houten, and Krenwinkel facing murder charges for the Tate and LaBianca killings. Tex Watson, who was arrested in Texas and fighting his extradition, received a separate trial in 1971.

At nine and a half months, the trial was among the longest and most expensive to date, according to numerous media accounts. But Manson and his girls keep things interesting, and newspapers around the world recounted every twist and turn. (There was so much publicity that, in order to keep the jury partial, Superior Court Judge Charles H. Older instituted a gag order that blocked access to trial transcripts and forbid lawyers and witnesses from talking to the press about matters other than evidence entered in open court.) Manson had wanted to represent himself, which Older did not allow. A lawyer named Irving Kanarek, who was known in the local law community as an obstructionist who strategically lengthened trials, was appealing enough to Manson. (Older would later sentence Kanarek to a night in jail for contempt to punish the lawyer's frequent interruptions.)

Because one is innocent until proven guilty, courts have long maintained that a defendant has the right to appear before a jury in civilian clothes, not a prison jumpsuit. The accused usually puts on a fresh shirt and shined shoes, trims their hair. Manson prepared for the opening day of his trial by carving an "X" in his forehead, between his eyes. He "Xed" himself off from the world and a society that didn't understand the method to his madness.

Atkins, Krenwinkel, and Van Houten followed suit, carving X's into their foreheads as well, and later shaving their heads. They walked into court holding hands and singing songs that Manson had written. Years later, Krenwinkel said these antics were orchestrated by Manson, who discussed how they could make a scene in court. Unruly and disruptive Family supporters were later banished from the courtroom and started holding a round-the-clock sidewalk vigil outside the Los Angeles House of Justice. Manson would stare at spectators in the gallery, and at one point, when the judge said Manson wasn't allowed to cross-examine a witness, leapt over the defense table and made a dash toward Older's bench, brandishing a pencil. Manson was dragged out kicking and screaming, yelling at Older "In the name of Christian justice, someone should chop off your head!" After the near attack, Older kept a .38 caliber revolver on his person during proceedings.

The state's star witness was Linda Kasabian, who drove the Manson Family to and from the Tate and LaBianca murders. "She never asked for immunity from prosecution, but we gave it," prosecutor Vincent Bugliosi said in a 2009 interview with the *Guardian*, adding that she sat on the witness stand for 17 or 18 days "and never broke down, despite the incredible pressure she was under." Since Manson did not physically participate in any of the murders he was being tried for, Bugliosi said that Kasabian's testimony was essential for the circumstantial conspiracy case. "I doubt we would have convicted Manson without her."

Another significant milestone of the trial happened in August 1970, when President Richard Nixon attended a Denver meeting of the federal Law Enforcement Assistance Administration. Crime had declined from the mid-1930s through the mid-1950s and increased quickly throughout the 1960s, with 1969 and 1970 seeing all-time high numbers of homicides. At the meeting, Nixon gave a speech that criticized Congress for failing to pass anti-crime legislation, announced his new federal efforts to fight crime, and complained about the media tendency to "glorify and to make heroes out of criminals." Then, he said something that just about everyone but Manson would regret: that Manson was "guilty, directly or indirectly, of eight murders without reason." The president started a firestorm by convicting Manson in the court of public opinion and refusing to take questions from reporters afterward. Nixon, who thought he said Manson was "charged" and not "guilty," painstakingly prepared a statement to clarify what he had said as his plane circled Andrews Air Force Base. Nonetheless, "MANSON GUILTY, NIXON DECLARES," graced the front page of the *Los Angeles Times* the next morning. Manson managed to get a copy from one of his lawyers, and later held it up for the jury to see. Manson's defense attorneys argued that the judge should declare a mistrial, but Older instead jailed one of Manson's lawyers for contempt of court.

The state rested their case after four months of witness testimony, and the defense then said they did not intend to call any witnesses. Atkins, Krenwinkel, and Van Houten had wanted to take the stand and put all the blame on themselves, prompting their lawyers to threaten to resign if Older allowed the women to incriminate themselves. (Manson would later give an hour-long speech to the court, without the jury present, saying that he was innocent and instructing his girls not to testify.)

Another twist in the trial came over the Thanksgiving recess, when Ronald Hughes, who was representing Leslie Van Houten, never returned from a camping trip. His body was found in a creek in Ventura County four months later. Van Houten's new attorney was given two weeks to catch up on the case, and then the trial continued with closing arguments.

Manson, Atkins, Krenwinkel, and Van Houten were found guilty on January 25, 1971, and sentenced to death. Their death row stint would be short, as the California Supreme Court banned capital punishment in February 1972, and the Manson Family sentences were commuted to life in prison. (The death penalty was reinstated a few months later through a voter referendum called Proposition 17, though California did not carry out another execution until 1992.)

Manson would later be convicted of two additional murders, of a musician named Gary Hinman and a Spahn ranch hand named Donald "Shorty" Shea. Manson and his followers, however, have said that they killed 35 people and buried them in the desert, a number that Bugliosi found high but quite possibly true.

PRISON IS MY HOME

Linda Kasabian went into hiding after the trial, living with a different name in a trailer park in the western United States. She has only given two interviews—the first on the trial of the century's twentieth anniversary.

"I could never accept the fact that I was not punished for my involvement," Kasabian told the *Guardian* in 2013. "I felt then what I feel now, always and forever, that it was a waste of life that had no reason, no rhyme."

No one involved in the Tate and LaBianca murders has ever been released from prison.

Susan Atkins died from brain cancer in 2009 at the Central California Women's Facility in Chowchilla. She became a born-again Christian shortly after entering prison and had been described as a model inmate who did outreach work. She was denied a compassionate release after a hearing in 2008, during which she read Psalm 23 and slept through much of the proceedings. The release was opposed by Sharon Tate's sister and Jay Sebring's nephew.

"I am incapable of hating. I commend them—always have commended them—for their good deeds that they have managed to accomplish within the walls of confinement," said Debra Tate. According to CNN, Tate has said that Atkins never offered her family an apology. "However, I do believe that the death of my sister, my nephew—which would be turning 40 years old right now, this week—is not an irrelevant cause."

Patricia Krenwinkel, now 71, and Leslie Van Houten, the youngest Manson murderer, who is now 69, have both come before the parole board numerous times. Van Houten, who earned bachelor's and master's degrees behind bars, was recommended for release by California's parole board in 2016 and 2017. As reported by *SF Gate*, Governor Jerry Brown considered the recommendation, taking into consideration

Van Houten's age and Manson's manipulation, but ended up rejecting the early release, writing in his decision that, even after five decades, Van Houten has not "wholly accepted responsibility for her role in the violent and brutal deaths of Mr. and Mrs. LaBianca."

Tex Watson is an ordained minister and another model prisoner who hasn't had any disciplinary issues since the 70s. His ministry, called "Abounding Love," maintains a website, though Watson does not have access to a computer and relies on others to update his content. On an FAQ page, Watson says that he is a committed vegetarian, to which he attributed his good health through the years. Watson also writes that during his yard time, he walks a track "sharing" his faith, or listens to Christian music or Bible talks on a radio.

Watson maintains his former leader was manipulative. "But I take full responsibility for my ignorance, lack of identity, emptiness, and choices in life, which left me prey to his deceptive plan. My actions were my own," Watson writes on his ministry's website.

Manson was a far less pious and well-behaved prisoner than his codefendants and was denied parole 12 times before his death at age 83 in November 2017. At some point along the way, he turned the X on his forehead into a swastika. A fellow inmate named Jan Holmstrom doused Manson in paint thinner then set him on fire in 1984, in the hobby shop at the California Medical Facility, a psychiatric prison. Manson suffered second- and third-degree burns on nearly 20 percent of his body, and the wounds were primarily on his face, hands, and scalp. Holmstrom later said he attacked Manson because the cult leader had been critical of his Hare Krishna beliefs.

Throughout his decades behind bars, Manson attempted to escape numerous times—including on a hot air balloon—and was cited for more than 100 disciplinary infractions that included throwing coffee in a guard's face, trying to flood part of his cellblock, setting his mattress on fire, and possessing weapons, cell phones, and drugs. In 2014, a gray-bearded Manson and his 27-year-old fiancée, Afton Elaine Burton, filed for a marriage license. The pair never tied the knot, and it later was revealed that Burton was working her magic to obtain and embalm Manson's body after his death, in hopes of enclosing it in a glass tomb for public viewing. Manson apparently called off the wedding after he realized that he was being conned (for once).

Manson grew to become a cultural icon to a new generation intrigued by his status as America's most famous criminal. In the late 1980s, a group of satanic worshippers chanted for his release outside of San Quentin. Manson's face adorns T-shirts, baseball hats, buttons, and coffee cups, his crazed grin familiar to generations who were born long after the summer of 1969.

"Most homicides and trials get a lot of attention and then fade," Bugliosi told the *Los Angeles Times*. Bugliosi died less than two years before Manson did. "Maniacs who kill to satisfy their urges do not resonate. Manson was different. As misguided as the murders were, he claimed that they were political and revolutionary, that he was trying to change the social order, not merely satisfy a homicidal urge. That appeals to the crazies on the fringes of society."

Manson continued to make headlines months after his death. There was no apparent successor, and Manson's body sat on ice in a top-secret location for several months as four men stepped forward to stake their claim. A California Superior Court judge eventually "awarded" Manson's body to Jason Freeman, a 41-year-old oil rigger from Florida who had only found out a few years earlier that he was Manson's grandson. According to *People*, Freeman, who was never able to meet his grandfather in person, said Manson would never kill a person carrying a baby, a reference to the slain pregnant actress Sharon Tate whose murder Manson was convicted of ordering. Freeman beat out Manson's longtime pen pal, his supposed son, and a memorabilia collector who hoped to walk away with Manson's remains.

Freeman held a private cremation ceremony for Manson in Porterville, California. About 25 people attended, including former Family member Sandra Good and would-be body snatcher Afton Elaine Burton. The funeral had a hippie vibe, according to Pastor Mark Pitcher, who gave a eulogy.

"He was born into an unhealthy environment to a 16-year-old girl who was not prepared for motherhood. He was a product of his environment, and that unhealthy environment followed him," Pitcher said while recounting his remarks to the *Porterville Recorder*. "Many choices were thrust upon Charlie as a young boy that had very damaging and destructive consequences upon him, and he made choices later on that were damaging and destructive to many for the rest of his life."

Mourners also sang songs written by Manson, as well as tunes by the Beach Boys and Guns N' Roses.

Spahn Ranch was once proposed as a tourist center or Christian daycare center, but neither of those plans materialized, and most of the property is now overgrown and owned by the state. After the murders of Tate and her friends, homeowner Rudolph Altobelli pursued *Life* magazine and Roman Polanski after the magazine published a photo of the grieving director on the front porch of the Cielo Drive house. Altobelli claimed the photo hurt the home's resale value. Future tenants, including Nine-Inch Nails musician Trent Reznor, didn't learn about the property's sordid history until they were ready to sign a lease agreement. The house was demolished in 1994 and replaced with a massive Mediterranean-style mansion. The LaBianca home still stands on Waverly Drive, but with a new address.

The only people more famous than Manson in this whole saga, as you might imagine, wanted nothing to do with the madman who turned their lyrics into an excuse for murdering innocent strangers. "You don't write songs for those reasons," Paul McCartney said in the *The Beatles Anthology* book in 2000.

JIM JONES AND THE PEOPLES TEMPLE OF THE DISCIPLES OF CHRIST

A young woman wears a multicolored dress with swirls of vibrant oranges, blues, and pinks, her slightly sweaty brow giving away the South American jungle heat. She's singing "That's the Way of the World," Earth, Wind and Fire's hit that topped the Billboard charts three years earlier. Children dance, and hundreds of people in the audience clap and sway with the beat.

Nearly everyone is captivated by the performance except the Reverend Jim Jones, the leader of the Peoples Temple of the

Disciples of Christ who had dreamed up this nearly 4,000-acre commune in Guyana. Jones wears a red shirt and dark glasses and chats with California Congressman Leo Ryan, who had arrived that day to check in on the nearly 1,000 people who had left San Francisco to live with Jones in the former British colony over the last year. Some of the formerly faithful had defected, escaping back to the United States with horrifying stories of Jones's abuse, as well as claims that their leader had confiscated passports and used other intimidation tactics to prevent others from leaving his "utopian" compound.

A sign behind the singer reads "Those who do not remember the past are condemned to repeat it." These words become all the more chilling when you realize that, less than 24 hours after this performance, just about everyone singing, dancing, clapping, and conversing will be dead. Some will be shot, but most will have taken a lethal dose of cyanide-laced grape Flavor Aid. Many drank the milky concoction voluntarily, even giving the poison to their own children. But not everyone was willing to "drink the Kool Aid," as the expression would later go. After knocking back the liquid, two "helpers" led cultists out of the pavilion—the same spot where they were laughing and celebrating just one night earlier—and laid them face-down on the earth to foam at the mouth and retch in pain for five excruciating minutes before dying. Those who resisted were either forcibly injected or shot. Their bodies would lie bloated, oozing, and decomposing for days on end in the South American summer heat before what was left of them was scraped up into a body bag, taken back to the country's capital, Georgetown, and finally transported back to the United States on military cargo jets.

At 912 deaths—913 if you count mastermind Jim Jones among the dead—Jonestown is by far the largest cult death that you'll read about in this book. In fact, Jonestown would remain the largest loss of American civilian life not related to a natural disaster until September 11, 2001. What makes Jonestown all the more tragic is the community's noble original mission: to create an equal society where people wouldn't be held back by the color of their skin or the social and economic situation that they had been dealt or born into.

Like those of any cult, members of the Peoples Temple didn't join Jim Jones because they dreamed of dying a horrible death in a strange country or because they wanted to be beaten and humiliated in front of their families and friends. Members previously held jobs that ranged from white collar professions, such as lawyers and medical workers, to housekeepers and waitstaff, to none at all. Those who joined the Peoples Temple, which combined Pentecostal Christianity and the revolutionary ideas from American culture in the 1960s and 1970s, followed Jones because they thought he was making a difference in the world. Peoples Temple institutions, such as free restaurants in Indiana, where the temple was founded, and later in San Francisco, provided meals to anyone who showed up. Starting in the early 1970s, the Peoples Temple three-story building on Geary Street in San Francisco's predominately black and underserved Fillmore District provided the community with a free health clinic and physical therapy center. Drug treatment and legal aid programs helped hundreds of people get clean and address their problems with the law and courts (according to the cult's numbers, which should always be taken with a grain of salt).

But in the end, Jones didn't practice what he preached. The man who once boasted that he had no need for more than one pair of shoes ordered his followers to hand over all their money and assets to the temple. Those who didn't have any cash often gave jewelry, furs—any worldly possessions of value—or would bake cakes for the church or do other odd jobs to ensure that they kept money flowing in. The reverend, who made his sleep-deprived followers listen for hours and hours as he denounced sex, actually slept with anyone he pleased. In Guyana, Jones ate meat while his overworked and nutrient-deprived followers ate rice that had maggots wriggling through the grains before it was cooked.

It's hard to say whether it was Jones's unbridled power, escalating mental illness, or drug addiction that pushed him from the light into the darkness. Maybe his intentions were never that holy. One thing is for certain: When Jones felt his socialist utopia was being threatened, it didn't take long for him to totally dismantle it, one human being at a time, until nearly 1,000 people were dead, far away from home.

JIM JONES'S EARLY YEARS

Jim Jones's father, James Thurman Jones, was born on May 13, 1931, in Crete, Indiana, and raised in the small nearby farming town of Lynn, where less than a thousand people lived. His mother, Lynetta Putnam, was a smart college dropout more interested in writing and progressive politics than homemaking. When in 1926 she married James T. Jones, who hailed from a wealthy family of landowners, Putnam thought she would finally put years of menial factory work behind her, as her new father-in-law owned a considerable amount of land in Richmond County.

But the buck stopped shortly after Jones's father put a down payment on a new home for the newlyweds. James T. Jones had a mental breakdown shortly after the birth of his son. A World War I veteran who had survived a German mustard gas attack with severely damaged lungs, Jones didn't have many lucrative work options (or the will to pursue them), and Lynette was left to pick up the slack. Little Jimmy Warren, as the future cult leader was called during his childhood, grew up with a father who spent his days at the pool hall on Main Street and a rabble-rousing, chain-smoking mother who wouldn't let him come back home until she had finished her shift at the Winchester Glass Factory. Myrtle Kennedy, an evangelical woman who took it upon herself to look after Jones in the afternoons, is credited with first taking Jones to church. Jones became enraptured with religion—in particular the Pentecostal Holy Rollers who spoke in tongues and rolled around on the floor to express their devotion to Christ.

Jones, a voracious and advanced reader from a young age, also had a propensity for preaching and a curious obsession with death. It wasn't uncommon for Jones's friends to find him out in the woods by himself, delivering a fiery sermon while standing on a tree stump. Around the time he was 10, Jones had built an altar in the attic of his family home. He would preach to his friends while dressed in a white sheet against the backdrop of candlelight. On one occasion, when one of Jones's friends disobeyed his orders during a sermon, the young reverend fetched his father's .22 caliber rifle and took a shot at the boy. Though Jones missed, he was still suspended from school and not allowed to see his friends for a while. Jones is often remembered as having a pack of stray animals following his every move, and some of his playmates have recounted that he tortured and killed animals in order to give them a proper funeral service and burial.

There were also the casket-factory break-ins. Jones's small hometown had a disproportionate number of companies that catered to the dead—five of the 13 local businesses manufactured coffins, according to a *New York Times* profile of Jones that was printed in the days following the massacre in Guyana. Most everyone in Lynn kept their doors unlocked, and the casket warehouse was not an exception. One night, Jones led a group of kids into the factory, instructing them to climb inside the coffins to experience for themselves what death might feel like. His accomplices were either too spooked or bored to come back with Jones, who kept returning to play dead.

The peculiarities didn't stop there. One time, Jones was convinced the Lord had instilled in him the power of flight. He leapt from the roof of a house, breaking his arm after falling to the ground. And while other boys in town pretended to be heroes while they played, Jones was more likely to emulate Adolf Hitler.

Tim Reiterman, a journalist who survived the ambush against Congressman Ryan and who later wrote *Raven: The Untold Story of the Rev. Jim Jones and His People*, has said that Jones "sought out acceptance and a family through churches but at the same time had a tremendous need for power and control."

"Good and evil coexisted in Jim Jones throughout his life. I really do believe, having gone back to his birthplace in Indiana and tracing his life, that the seeds of the madness that the world saw in November 1978 were there from his earliest years," Reiterman said in an interview with *Time* on the thirtieth anniversary of the Jonestown massacre.

By the time he was a teenager, Jones had given his first sermon at a Pentecostal church and was preaching on street corners. And at his high school, Jones's future interest in communism, already influenced by his mother's left-leaning politics at home, was taking root. Jones joined the Christian Youth Fellowship, where the idea of compassionate and equal churches, and what members called "Christian communism," was often the topic of conversation.

James T. Jones was dead before his son turned 18. Stepping up to provide for his family, Jones started working nights at Reid Memorial Hospital while still attending high school during the day. There, Jones met a senior nursing student and his future wife, Marceline Baldwin. Marceline and Jones crossed paths as she was preparing a dead body to be picked up by a funeral director. Apparently, she was impressed by the warmth and compassion that Jones showed to the bereaved.

Jones went away to college the following year to study education. During his university years, Jones, who had no formal training aside from ministering to dead animals, tree stumps, and at Pentecostal revivals, opened a church of his own in Indianapolis (funded, in part, by his side hustle as a door-to-door salesman hawking imported South American monkeys). Jones's message of integration resonated with the diverse congregation during a time that preceded Dr. Martin Luther King Jr. and the Civil Rights era, when the Ku Klux Klan was still very active in Indiana. Jim and Marceline Jones began growing what they would call their "rainbow family." They went on to have seven children total: one biological son, Stephan Gandhi Jones, and six adopted black, Native American, and Korean children. The Joneses were the first white family in the state to adopt a black child, whom they named James Warren Jones Jr., and this distinction led to hurtful and racist taunts and spitting at Marceline when she went out in public with the children.

Jones became paranoid in the coming years, as was evident in the early Peoples Temple days in Indianapolis. He suspected that his food was being poisoned and his phone lines were tapped by the CIA. Around 1961, Jones started believing that Indianapolis would be the target of a nuclear attack—not a totally out-there assumption, as the United States was in the Cold War with the Soviet Union. Around that time, *Esquire* had printed a story listing the nine safest spots in America. At the top of the list was Eureka, California, a coastal city about 270 miles north of San Francisco. Four years later, Jones moved the Peoples Temple west, settling in the Redwood Valley outside of Ukiah, California, about 167 miles south of Eureka.

THE PEOPLES TEMPLE RISES

Money was scarce as the Peoples Temple grew roots in California. Jones, who had graduated with a degree in education, taught adult education classes in Ukiah to bring in money.

New members eventually started coming. They might have attended one of Jones's lively services and watched him cast cancer out of an audience member's body (a feat that was a carefully orchestrated inside job, complete with a secret stash of chicken gizzards and other organs). Jones attracted a wide range of people, from idealists who wanted to make the world a better place to addicts, drunks, and other down-and-out types who were moved by Jones's power to make them feel special.

It was one of these healings that led Elmer Mertle to quit his job at Standard Oil, sell the family home, and move up to Ukiah in 1969. Mertle's wife, Deanna, believed that Jones had telepathically cured her 17-year-old son of (an undiagnosed) heart condition.

In a story that appeared in the magazine *New West*, Deanna recalled Jones being compassionate to old people and tender to the children during the early days. But this compassion eventually gave way to mental punishment and then escalated to physical, public beatings, first with a belt, then a paddle, then a large wooden instrument that Jones called "the board of education." Elmer Mertle recalled Jones's demeanor after a public punishment:

> *Jim would then come over and put his arms around the person and say, "I realize that you went through a lot, but it was for the cause. Father loves you and you're a stronger person now. I can trust you more now that you've gone through this and accepted this discipline."*

The Mertles recounted rationalizing the beatings because of the praise that Jones always followed up with. A turning point came, however, after the Mertles' 16-year-old daughter Linda was paddled 75 times for hugging and kissing a female friend who was believed to be a lesbian. Jones disciplined her as six or seven hundred people looked on, according to her parents. The beating was so bad that Linda's backside looked like hamburger meat, and the teen couldn't sit down for more than a week. Despite seeing their daughter brutally beaten and humiliated, the Mertles stayed on with the Peoples Temple for another year. They had no money, no jobs, and nowhere else to live.

"We had nothing on the outside to get started in," Elmer Mertle said. "We had given [the church] all our money. We had given all our property. We had given up our jobs."

(The Mertles, who had also signed power of attorney papers over to the church, had to legally change their names to Al and Jeannie Mills when they left Peoples Temple in 1974. The Mertles/Mills became vocal critics of Jones and operated a halfway house called the Human Freedom Center that was open to Peoples Temple survivors and other cult defectors. In February 1980, the Mills were found murdered in their home along with their daughter, Daphne. Rumors swirled that a Peoples Temple "hit squad" was behind the homicides, or that Eddie Mills, the same son whom they believed Jones healed, was to blame, as he was the only person at home during the triple murder who wasn't killed. Eddie Mills was detained in 2005 but never arrested for the murders, which remain unsolved.)

Peoples Temple members were also expected to give 25 percent of their earnings to the church, a practice conventionally called tithing that Jones referred to as "the commitment." The Mertles had property to give. Those who didn't have a job or assets handed over furs, watches, their time, and anything of value.

Despite Jones's increasingly violent behavior, the church continued to attract hard-working altruistic people who wanted to make a difference in the world and who shared Jones's socialist ideals. A large percentage of the Peoples Temple congregation was black, and Jones vowed to provide them with access to the jobs, education, and other opportunities—an appealing prospect as the United States was in the midst of the Civil Rights Movement. The church expanded in the coming years, holding services in San Francisco starting in 1970 and purchasing a three-story building on Geary Street in the Fillmore neighborhood that housed the temple, free clinic, canteen, and drug treatment center.

But guards patted down parishioners before they entered the church. Jones might be flanked by up to 15 bodyguards at a time. Visitors—even high-profile California politicians whom the Peoples Temple helped elect through letter-writing campaigns, canvassing, and other shows of force—were discouraged from dropping by unannounced.

And, even though the Sunday offerings brought in thousands of dollars, Jones said only hundreds were coming in. Where was all the money going?

MAKING IT BIG

The Peoples Temple rapidly expanded in the 1970s, opening up a third location in a former synagogue on South Alvarado Street in Los Angeles in 1971. The following year, there was a massive recruitment effort. Peoples Temple members spent the weekends on marathon bus trips, boarding in Ukiah and driving to San Francisco for a day-long temple meeting. Back on the bus, they slept through the night on a ride down to Los Angeles, where another full-day service awaited them. They crammed back on the buses, which were often at double capacity, to head home after a whirlwind weekend. Jones, meanwhile, spread out in the back of the number seven Peoples Temple bus, which had been tricked out with a bed, refrigerator, sink, and steel plate to protect him against attackers. Jones kept the cash back there as well.

Grace Stoen, a former high-ranking Peoples Temple member who kept records for the temple businesses, says Jones's motivation for opening additional temples was all about the money.

"Jim would say, 'If we stay here in the valley, we're wasted. We could make it to the big-time in San Francisco,'" Stoen recalled in a *New West* article, saying that an urban temple could bring his cult up to $25,000 a weekend in the offering plate.

The Peoples Temple also had tremendous political sway. With its sheer number of followers, Peoples Temple could influence local elections. Even during the early days in Ukiah, Jones reportedly managed to control nearly 16 percent of the vote during off-year elections. The political power of the Peoples Temple only increased when it got to San Francisco. Jones's followers are credited with helping elect progressive leaders such as San Francisco Mayor George Moscone and City Supervisor Harvey Milk through rallies, canvassing, and voting for them. Jones organized mass voting fraud, sending his followers to different areas of California to vote for the candidate that the cult was backing. Jones was rewarded for his efforts with a position on San Francisco's Housing Authority in 1976, and was later named chairman. The Peoples Temple hosted dinner for high-ranking California dignitaries, and Jones counted Governor Jerry Brown among his friends. Those who questioned Jones's odd church were advised to keep their opinions to themselves.

But while Jones was shaking hands, making allies, and infiltrating San Francisco city government, even more disturbing things were going on behind the scenes. In 1973, Jones started holding what would become known as "suicide drills" after several members defected from the temple. One member recalled Jones telling the crowd at the evening meeting that they were going to celebrate that night, and paper cups with wine were passed out. After everyone had finished, Jones informed them that they had just drunk poison that would kill them in 30 minutes. When a half hour passed and no one died, Jones told them that this had just been a drill that he thought up to test their loyalty. Apparently, they passed.

ESCAPE TO SOUTH AMERICA

We're going to have to get our heads out of the sky and realize that if we want heaven, we'll have to build it here, on Earth, for ourselves.

—Jim Jones, Peoples Temple press release

On August 1, 1977, Jones fled to Guyana just hours before a negative article about him and the Peoples Temple was set to hit newsstands in *New West*. Twelve former members bravely went on record in "Inside Peoples Temple," where they shared their firsthand account and insights into Jones's fake healings, marathon meetings that would last until the sun came up, physical and mental abuse, and financial hoarding, which included pilfering government money that was supposed to be used for a school for emotionally disturbed boys. Journalists Marshall Kilduff and Phil Tracy described life in Jones's world as "a mixture of Spartan regimentation, fear, and self-imposed humiliation."

Jones wasn't the only one who wanted to stop the presses: The *New West* offices received some 50 phone calls and 70 letters per day leading up to the publication, including a message from California's lieutenant governor Mervyn Dymally to leave Jones alone. "He's a good man who does good work" was the spirit of many of the communications.

Once Jones left the US, Peoples Temple members quickly followed him south to Guyana. They packed up under the cover of darkness, many of them leaving without telling their families where exactly they'd be going, or why. There was unbelievable excitement among temple members, who were thrilled at the opportunity to go to Jonestown, this paradise community with so much potential. Upon arrival, they handed over their passports, money, jewelry, social security checks, and any other valuables to Jonestown officials.

Jones had leased 3,800 acres in Guyana, the only English-speaking and socialist country in South America, a few years earlier. He had a 25-year lease on the land, and, after some bartering, ended up paying 25 cents an acre. He was also cozy with higher-ups in the Guyanese government, which allowed

Jonestown boats to bypass Guyanese customs to bring in produce and supplies.

The terrain was rugged, and there was much work to be done to build the compound, officially called The Peoples Temple Agricultural Project. Luckily for Jones, he had about a thousand people whom he could trust (or control) to cut wood, drive tractors, and do the heavy weeding necessary to get the community up and running.

Some former members recall those early days in Guyana as fresh, exciting, and full of potential.

"Everything was new and unique, and just fun, you know, we just had fun with it as it grew. I just loved that we created what we ate, that we did all these jobs," recalled Laura Johnston Kohl in the documentary *Jonestown: The Life and Death of Peoples Temple*.

Odell Rhodes, one of the few people who managed to escape the Jonestown massacre after it started, later reflected on the early days positively as well. "It was the hardest work I ever had. But it wasn't as though you just waited for the day to be over. You were at work with all your friends, and you knew that the work you did would bring food to the people you liked. I didn't mind. I was happy with the work," Rhodes said in the 1981 book *Awake in a Nightmare: Jonestown, the Only Eyewitness Account*.

Jim Jones Jr., Jones's adopted son and namesake, recalled the new community as an opportunity for African Americans from impoverished backgrounds to finally be shareholders in a community.

But behind the smiling faces of Jonestown residents in early photos and footage was an isolated world controlled by Jim Jones. Days were regimented, with lights on at 6 a.m. Breakfast consisted of rice, watery milk, and brown sugar. Everyone at Jonestown had a task, and those working in the fields might have had to walk an hour and a half in 100-degree heat and then work for 10 hours, subsisting on little more than their nutrient-free breakfast and more rice for lunch. After putting in a full day of labor, they'd make the trek back to their homes, take cold showers (Jonestown lacked flush toilets, too), and eat dinner (more rice, perhaps mixed with wild greens). Russian language lessons started after dinner, as Jones often contemplated moving the Peoples Temple to the Soviet Union as a way to put more space between them and the hostile United States.

Adam Lusher reports in the *Independent* that Peoples Forum meetings were held up to three times a week, sometimes continuing until 3 a.m., with Jones denouncing sex as animalistic, doling out public humiliations, beratings, and beatings, and working to instill his paranoia in his followers. They couldn't go back to the US, he said, because people were trying to get rid of blacks and Native Americans. Guyana was their only hope. Exhausted and depleted, Jones's followers would return to their small wood cottages, with beds crammed together for maximum capacity, to get what little sleep they could and start all over again at 6 a.m.

Leaving wasn't an option. When community members expressed an interest to go, or that they were homesick, Jones would clutch his chest and act as if he were having a heart attack. Temple members were encouraged to inform on others who were talking about leaving. Snitches were rewarded, and those who had been turned in for contemplating an escape were taken to the "Extra Care Unit," where they would be drugged, sometimes for weeks at a time, and come back a shell of their former selves. Armed guards patrolled the commune's exits and surrounding trails, while sentries kept watch from a tower (which, strangely enough, was painted with yellow fish and doubled as a children's slide on a lower level). But there wasn't any barbed wire surrounding the complex. Jones had done everything else to ensure that his members would stay within Jonestown.

As time went on, Jones appeared to become sicker and sicker. He was even more paranoid, thinking he'd been shot at from the woods, or poisoned. He would stumble more, and slur his words, returning to his wood house—slightly bigger than all the other shacks—and return amped up and full of energy. The extent of Jones's drug addiction wouldn't be uncovered until after the massacre, when reporters on a tour of the compound would find needles, morphine, hundreds of Valium pills, and barbiturates in Jones's medicine cabinet.

As the days at Jonestown went on, family members and friends that Peoples Temple members had left behind grew increasingly concerned. Several lawsuits were filed by parents trying to get their children back from Guyana. A Concerned Relatives group formed. Jones deployed what he called "white nights." During these white nights, Peoples Temple members were woken up by sirens and told to quickly congregate in the pavilion. Inside, they were instructed to drink what they were told was poison. A few hours after the suicide drill started, Jones's voice would come on over the loudspeaker, declaring that this was just a test to see who was loyal to him. In May 1978, a high-ranking aide named Deborah Layton escaped. Layton would later say in a deposition that during these white nights, Jones told them that they were surrounded by enemies that would torture them if they were captured, and to drink the poison. They did as they were told.

The Concerned Relatives group had the ear of Congressman Leo Ryan, who represented San Mateo County and was concerned that his constituents were being held against their will and that Jones was stockpiling ammunition. With great preparations, Ryan left to see Jonestown for himself, accompanied by a delegation that included reporters and his aides.

Ryan's group arrived in Jonestown on November 17, 1978, without any protection from the military or the State Department, even though they had reason to expect violence. They toured the Peoples Temple vegetable gardens, medical clinic, and daycare, and were impressed by the amount of work and dedication it had taken to build this community from the ground up. To round out the evening, Peoples Temple members performed in the pavilion, and Ryan told the crowd that from what he had learned so far, some people believed Jonestown was the best thing that ever happened to them.

But something very sinister was brewing under the smiles, cheers, and press photo ops.

NOVEMBER 18, 1978

Jonestown survivors remember the day starting off as sunny, with black clouds, a rainstorm, and high winds suddenly and swiftly blowing through. Journalists were conducting interviews, and Tim Reiterman recalled Jones's sallow skin and weak handshake. "When he spoke, there was a constant undercurrent of paranoia," Reiterman said in *Time*. "He even seemed to put a figurative gun in the hands of us journalists, saying we don't need to shoot him, that our words have that kind of effect. He was clearly viewing himself as a martyr and it was very bothersome to realize that over 900 lives were in the hands of this man."

All the while, notes were being passed to reporters asking for help to get out of Jonestown, and several temple members told Ryan's legislative counsel, Jackie Speier, that they wanted to be on the plane out of Jonestown with the congressman. Although Jones claimed in interviews that anyone was free to leave, this was clearly not the case, and as his dissatisfaction grew, the scene grew more chaotic. More people stepped up, saying they wanted to flee the jungle "utopia" as well. As emotions peaked, a man named Don Sly pulled out a knife and attempted to stab Ryan. Sly ended up stabbing his own hand in the process, and footage later showed Ryan emerging from the pavilion with visible blood stains on his shirt. Although Ryan was supposed to spend the night in Jonestown, he left with the group of defectors for the Port Kaituma airstrip six miles away.

While the group waited for the airplane to leave, a tractor trailer pulled up with Peoples Temple guards wielding guns. The congressman and others searched for shelter on the tarmac, hiding behind tires or lying flat, pretending to be dead. Ryan was shot more than 20 times and died at the airstrip alongside news reporters and crew members Bob Brown, Don Harris, and Greg Robinson. Speier, who was shot at point-blank range, lay wounded with nine others who were left for dead and not rescued until 22 hours after the attack. As the chaos unfolded outside, one of the defectors already on the airplane, Larry Layton, pulled out a handgun and opened fire, shooting two escapees and attempting to fire at a third.

THE MASSACRE

Back at Jonestown, Jones's wife, Marceline, advised everyone to calm down and get some rest in their cabins. But before too long, a message came over the loudspeaker: report to the pavilion immediately. When everyone had assembled, Jones told his followers that he'd had a premonition: Someone on the airplane would shoot and kill Congressman Ryan, sending the plane crashing down. He didn't know how, or why, but he knew it was going to happen. Jones told them the Guyanese Defense Force was en route to Jonestown and would start shooting and torturing people within the hour. In addition, he told them Ryan's death would only mean more scrutiny for their community. The Americans would be coming, too, and everything would be ruined. The only choice they had left, according to Jones, was to "die with respect, die with a degree of dignity." But he also gave his followers a chance to speak up if they disagreed with his fatal plan.

One woman named Christine Miller threw in her dissenting voice, asking if it was too late to be airlifted to Russia. Jones, sounding exacerbated, told her he was trying to get Russia on the phone. "What more do you suggest?" he snapped on the so-called "death tape" recording made that day.

"When we destroy ourselves, we're defeated. We let them, the enemies, defeat us," Christine Miller said. "I look at all these babies and I think they deserve to live."

From there, Miller's will to live and to leave was shot down by the group, who began shouting at her. With armed guards surrounding the pavilion, Jones called upon the Peoples Temple doctor, Lawrence Schacht, to start administering "the medication."

A large stainless-steel tub was brought into the pavilion, filled with the milky-white Flavor Aid laced with cyanide. The babies and children, given the poison first, were either spoon-fed or had the liquid squirted down their throats. "Mother, mother, mother, mother, please," Jones pleaded, asking women to not resist and bring their children forward. Adults were given a cup of the potion. Those who refused were held down and forced to drink or injected with the cyanide. After receiving their dose, Peoples Temple members were guided out of the pavilion by two others and placed facedown on the ground. This wasn't a humane act that allowed people to die outside in nature, on the ground they had cleared with their own hands; rather, it was an orderly process to dole out poison without being slowed down by the dying. It was a death assembly line, Henry Ford style.

As time passed, Jones encouraged his followers to meet death, telling them that "death is just stepping over into another plane" and that good communists died with dignity, not in hysterics.

One by one, hundreds of people took the poison, including more than 300 children. Whether anyone truly took their dose voluntarily is up for debate. They spent five agonizing minutes holding each other, convulsing, retching in pain, and gasping for air before they took in their last breath in jungle of South America. Jones, 46, would be found, not with his people in the mud, but on the pavilion stage near the chair where he gave his sermons, a fatal bullet wound under his right ear.

AFTERMATH

The bodies of the Jonestown victims would lie bloated, oozing, and decomposing for days until forces arrived to scrape up what was left of them into body bags.

Only a handful of survivors were able to escape from Jonestown once the massacre had started. A group of 11 Peoples Temple members hiked 30 miles through the jungle, including Leslie Wagner-Wilson, who made the trek with her three-year-old son, Jakari, strapped to her back. Odell Rhodes, who taught arts and crafts to the Jonestown children, managed to escape the horror when Dr. Schacht asked him to fetch a stethoscope. One survivor hid out in a ditch; another woman fell asleep while taking cover under her bed, waking up the next day. Humans were not the only beings to perish that day; cats and dogs—even the Jonestown mascot, a chimpanzee named Mr. Muggs—were shot and killed.

Other Peoples Temple members survived because they were away on temple business that fateful day. Jim Jones Jr. was at a basketball tournament in Georgetown, Guyana's capital city, when he got a call over the radio that something went down. Three other men were instructed to take half a million dollars in cash to the Soviet embassy in Georgetown after the chaos started earlier that day.

Three days after the massacre, responding Guyanese troops estimated the Jonestown death toll at around 400. The United States sent hundreds of troops down as well, and helicopters flew over the jungle, calling out to potential survivors over a loudspeaker. But just a dozen or so people were found in the jungle, and after a few days US officials began to wonder if hundreds of people really had managed to escape Jones's final solution.

Then, on November 25, US officials said the responding Guyanese troops made a horrifying discovery: There were more uncounted dead bodies to be found layered underneath the visible corpses.

"We simply began to discover more and more and more bodies," Air Force Captain John J. Moscatelli was reported to say in the *Washington Post*. "Under adults we found smaller adults and children, and more small babies than anticipated."

It would take emergency responders eight days to pack the bodies in plastic bags. Just nine autopsies were performed in Guyana, including Congressman Ryan's, and the Guyanese government made an exception to a law that required the rest to be autopsied. Remains were packed into aluminum coffins and transported via cargo planes back to Dover Air Force Base in Delaware. The bodies that were able to be identified were released to their families; the remains of 248 others would eventually be buried in a mass grave at Evergreen Cemetery in Oakland, California.

Survivors of Jonestown and the Port Kaituma attacks were taken to the Park Hotel in Georgetown which, by the following week, was swarming with reporters from around the world.

"The survivors, some of them children, stared at the reporters with vacant, ancient eyes. There were literally hundreds of journalists from at least five continents in Georgetown. It was madness. Virulent lunacy. And when you tried to assemble bits and pieces of the story, none of it fit together. There was no perspective, no center," *Rolling Stone* journalist Tim Cahill wrote about the scene at the hotel.

About 85 survivors stayed in Guyana—either at the hotel or at the Peoples Temple house—for about a month before flying back to the United States. Once the survivors landed in New York, they met federal agents who were waiting to question them. Their passports were seized, and they had to pay a repatriation fee.

In the days following the massacre, about 25 Peoples Temple members who were still living in San Francisco took refuge in the locked Geary Street headquarters. On November 20, relatives waiting to hear about the fate of their loved ones went to the temple. According to an Associated Press report, a woman named Margie Henderson pounded on the fence, yelling "Where's my mother? ... Shoot me! Shoot me like you shot them!"

By the time journalists were cleared to travel to Jonestown, the smell of death was so overpowering that it could be detected inside the airplane, 300 feet in the air. Charles Krause of the *Washington Post* said that Jonestown from the sky "literally looked like a garbage dump where somebody dumped a lot of rag dolls." The press corps toured Jones's home, rifling through books and magazines about communism and conspiracies, his well-stocked medicine cabinet, and his collection of self-analysis letters addressed to "Dad."

Marceline Jones also died in Guyana, and her parents back in Indiana handled the funeral arrangement for their daughter and the deposed reverend. Ernest Mills from Doan & Mills Funeral Home in Richmond, Indiana, recalled that when the Joneses' funeral was being planned, Peoples Temple members from California were planning to charter buses to come and mourn. The FBI wanted a layout of the building for security purposes. Because of all the fuss, Jones's ashes were ultimately scattered at sea, while his wife's remains were buried in Indiana's Earlham Cemetery without fanfare.

At the time, Jonestown was considered an act of mass suicide. But as more information came out, the victims of Jonestown have been considered murder victims more so than willing participants.

Larry Layton was the only Peoples Temple member to be tried for the events of November 18, 1978. After his first trial ended in a hung jury, Layton was convicted of four charges in March 1987: conspiracy and aiding and abetting in the shootings of Congressman Ryan and Richard C. Dwyer, deputy chief of the US Mission in Guyana (who had been shot at the airstrip but survived); conspiracy to commit Ryan's murder; and conspiring to attack Dwyer. He was sentenced to mandatory life terms for the conspiracy murder charge. His family, Peoples Temple members, and cult scholars petitioned President Bill Clinton for a pardon, which never materialized. Layton was eventually granted early release and left a federal prison in 2002. He reportedly lives in northern California.

Jackie Speier, Ryan's legislative aide who took cover under the wheel of the plane on the Port Kaituma airstrip, is now Representative Jackie Speier. She has held Ryan's congressional seat since 2008.

Jim Jones Jr. would spend the first 15 years after Jonestown going by the name "James Jones." He told talk show host Oprah Winfrey that he forgives his father, who suffered from mental illness, drug abuse, and unchecked power.

"Nine hundred people died, and I miss them every day. But I also recognize that they tried. They tried something—they failed horrifically—but they tried, and out of that, I've taken a lot of pride to realize that I'm Jim Jones Jr. I can't hide from that," he said in 2010.

Down in Guyana, Jonestown has largely been viewed as an American problem, and the incident never received a government investigation. A story on the tenth anniversary reported that the Ministry of Information had only recently started helping arrange visits to the site, and it wasn't until 2009 that the Guyanese Tourism Authority erected a plaque commemorating the victims. No one has ever tried to rebuild or settle on the site out of fear—though there have been talks of redeveloping Jonestown as a dark tourism site that could bring in much-needed tourism dollars to the impoverished area. Many locals believe Jonestown is haunted by evil spirits of Caribbean lore, called *jumbies*.

Despite Jones's intentions and abuse, the commune was a hopeful experience, full of promise for so many and a place where they could work to make the world a better place. In the decades since, the jungle has reclaimed the hundreds of acres that were so quickly and lovingly cleared. A decade after the massacre, only a few of the pavilion's support poles remain. None of the hundred or so buildings survived, and abandoned equipment has gathered rust. The site where nearly a thousand bodies lay dead for days before being rescued from the elements, has been covered in weeds and a bougainvillea bush that left the charnel ground in a "cascade of bright purple," William R. Long reported in the *Los Angeles Times*.

CHAPTER 4

ROCH THÉRIAULT AND HIS ANT HILL KIDS

With a long, black beard, piercing blue eyes, and simple clothes, Roch Thériault certainly looked the part of an Old Testament prophet. Thériault even had members of his Christian doomsday cult call him Moses. But he was nothing like the heroic figure to whom God appeared as a burning bush on Mount Horeb and instructed to lead the Israelites out of Egypt to the land of milk and honey. Unless Moses was an alcoholic, took eight wives, and doled out severe corporeal punishment that included pulled teeth, severed limbs, and disembowelment, but those particular Bible stories don't ring a bell.

Thériault had a small group of followers—eight women, two men, and 28 children (most of whom he had fathered). Cult members, whom Thériault referred to as the Ant Hill Kids, believed that their leader was taking them to the promised land. From 1977 to 1989, Thériault turned this band of followers, who initially joined him because they were interested in living a healthier life, into a sequestered group waiting out doomsday in the rural Canadian woods. The supposed day of the apocalypse came and went, and with the passing years, Thériault kept an even tighter—and brutally abusive—grip on the men, women, and children who depended on him to have their basic needs met.

Roch Thériault was on the radar of law enforcement and social services for years before he became one of Canada's most notorious cult leaders. But Thériault's maniacal ways would not be stopped for good until multiple Ant Hill Kids were dead and one of his many wives managed to escape, emerging from the woods clinging to life, missing her right arm.

BECOMING MOSES

Roch Thériault, born on May 16, 1947, grew up poor in the small Canadian mining town of Thetford Mines, Quebec, about 65 miles south of Quebec City. Thériault was a charismatic, well-read student who didn't advance beyond the seventh grade, the highest offered at the local four-room schoolhouse. Even after he killed, maimed, and tortured his followers, he was described by a psychiatrist as a "Renaissance man" who possessed a "bright, inquisitive, and sensitive nature."

His family belonged to a Roman Catholic movement called the Pilgrims of St. Michael. They were also known as the "white berets" and were easily identified by the hats they wore while going door to door to hand out literature on the group's mission, which promoted a "more Christian society" by advocating for a more equitable class structure and the disbandment of powerful banks. Thériault begrudgingly proselytized with his family, which fueled his lifelong hate of the Catholic church.

By the early 1970s, Thériault was bankrupt and out of work, with a wife and two young children to care for. An ulcer surgery had left him in constant pain and with digestion issues. In the face of these hopeless and seemingly incurable complications, Thériault became obsessed with reading about medicine and religion, and joined the Seventh-day Adventist church in his hometown. A Protestant denomination with apocalyptic roots, Seventh-day Adventists encouraged vegetarian eating and clean living long before the rest of Western society caught on to the craze. Thériault's humor and charming demeanor impressed church leaders, and he was soon leading a class on how to quit smoking. But Thériault was on the outs with his new brethren just as quickly as he ascended, with church leadership finding him too arrogant and kicking him out.

Though his time with the Adventists was brief, Thériault had been around long enough to attract a band of vulnerable spiritual seekers who were interested in branching off with him.

Gabrielle Lavallée was among his recruits. Lavallée, who had trained as a nurse but in recent years had turned to stripping to fuel her drug addiction, was in a deep depression and looking for meaning in her life when she and a friend found work at a Seventh-day Adventist retreat.

"I was wondering who I really was, I wondered what I was doing on Earth, I was wondering where I was coming from," Lavallée recalled in a documentary directed by Lynn Booth. "I didn't have very much confidence in myself, I didn't believe in myself." But things started to make sense as soon as she and Thériault crossed paths. She felt at ease in his presence and "immediately poured out her story," wrote journalists Paul Kaihla and Ross Laver in *Savage Messiah*. "She wasn't particularly proud of everything she had done, but over the years she experienced many strange dreams and visions which seemed to indicate that there was a higher purpose to her life. Once, lying in bed at night, she had looked up at the ceiling and had seen a bright light, in which stood a man dressed in a tunic" who looked just like Thériault—a sign that "destiny had brought them together."

Thériault, who at that time already said he was directly conversing with God, saw something in Lavallée. He was starting a natural healing center and asked Lavallée to join him, telling her that this would be a once-in-a-lifetime opportunity to serve others. Lavallée agreed, never dreaming that she would spend the next 11 years of her life with a false and maniacal prophet.

Once up and running, Thériault's center offered the most alternative of alternative treatments, including a grape juice prescription for leukemia that ultimately led to the death of the woman who had taken his holistic advice. But by the summer of 1978, Thériault believed he had a different responsibility. God was warning him that the end of the world was fast approaching, and even gave Thériault a date to get ready for: February 17, 1978. Thériault believed that he and his group would survive the apocalypse if they took refuge in the forest and that he would be responsible for rebuilding a new world out of the rubble. Thériault and a group of nine women, four men, and a few children set off to eastern Quebec to prepare for the end times—and what was to come after.

SETTING UP CAMP

The Ant Hill Kids, who were given this name by Thériault for their hard and steadfast work, wasted no time clearing the thick Canadian woods in the Gaspé Peninsula ahead of a long and harsh winter. The group arrived in early July and lived in tents until they built a communal log cabin tailored to Thériault's specifications.

They especially resembled a colony of ants that first week, when they were up by 5 a.m. hiking to the main road to fetch food and supplies from their cars. They felled trees with chainsaws and worked long after sunset. Their meals were strictly rationed and consisted of little more than raw vegetables. Members of the cult would later recall that during those early days in the woods, they were mostly focused on if they would have enough food to eat that night for dinner. Had they been better fed and rested, they might have been able to notice the drastic change in Thériault—who had started lecturing the group long into the night on the corrupt nature of society and evilness of conventional families, and forcing the Ant Hill Kids to share stories of their childhoods.

"We always tried to denigrate our parents because our parents were supposed to be bad," recalled a former member, Marise

Lambert, in an interview with a Canadian magazine. "Our parents didn't give us good things." Good things, Lambert said, could only come from Thériault.

The cabin was completed after a month of backbreaking work. To symbolize this next chapter in the wilderness away from society, Thériault christened each of his followers with Biblical names. Gabrielle Lavallée became Tirza, one of four sisters the Old Testament permitted by God to inherit their father's land. Thériault's wife, Gisèle, became known as Esther, a heroic queen who saved the Jews from mass slaughter in ancient Persia. And Thériault humbly saved the name Moses, the Old Testament hero who led his people out of the darkness and into the light, for himself.

As the Ant Hill Kids settled into life in the wilderness, it was clear that Thériault was not sticking to his clean-eating, holistic roots (not to mention that he didn't seem to have the moral compass expected of a religious leader). He ate meat, drank soda, and snacked on potato chips. Some of these culinary delights were donated to the group in the woods by local residents, but Thériault also pimped out one of the Ant Hill women to a local shopkeeper in exchange for provisions.

That autumn, when Thériault's wife Gisèle/Esther was about six months pregnant, he started taking the other women as spiritual wives, citing the Biblical story of King David, the second king of Israel and Judah (and of David and Goliath fame), who married at least seven women and also kept concubines. Thériault grew his harem over a period of months, and years later with the help of a polygamist in Utah, held marriage ceremonies with many of his "wives" in absentia. Thériault soon started pitting the numerous women he was sleeping with against each other to fight for his attention. Thériault was believed to have fathered 28 cult children.

February 17, 1978, came and went. When the rest of the world didn't crumble around them, Thériault attributed this minor detail to God having a different clock than mere mortals. And so the group continued on at the mercy of Thériault, whose mood could change in an instant, depending on the weather that day or how much he had been drinking. He disciplined his children by pinning them against a tree with a knife and instructing their mothers to throw rocks at them, and worked his followers ragged to create his vision of a divine existence, subjecting them to his teachings and drunken rages.

Michael Kropveld, the founder and director of the Canadian nonprofit Info-Cult, has described the evolution of cults such as Thériault's Ant Hill Kids as an escalating process. "In the case of Thériault, you can see that because he could do what he wanted and no one reacted against it, what was to stop it from going further."

THE FIRST DEATH

Thériault's power would go unchecked for two more years, when Canadian authorities caught wind of a horrifying incident.

On March 23, 1981, 2-year-old Samuel Giguère wouldn't stop crying. His parents, Jacques Giguère and Maryse Grenier, were out in the woods working that day, and their toddler was being watched by Guy Veer, a former patient who had been treated for depression in a mental hospital. He was responsible for baby-sitting children while their parents toiled away for Thériault.

"I was really mad," Veer would later testify when recalling that day. "Each time I started to doze off, he started blubbering."

Veer's solution was to hit the toddler in the face more than five times to shut him up. Gabrielle Lavallée, the resident nurse, would care for the boy over the next few days, and testified that Samuel was unable to sit up on his own or eat solid foods.

Two days after the beating, Lavallée noticed the toddler had an egg-sized swelling on his penis that was preventing him from urinating, and Thériault insisted on taking the surgical lead. Using a pair of sterilized scissors, Thériault made an incision to drain the lump, and Lavallée applied a paste she had made from iodine, olive oil, and plantain. The following day, Samuel was so sick that he had to be fed fluids a drop at a time. The boy died three days after he was beaten. In a final tender act, Thériault and the boy's parents decided to burn the toddler's body so that his corpse wouldn't be eaten by wild animals when buried outside.

At least, that's the story that witnesses told police and the courts at the time. Kaihla and Laver write that Thériault likely had tried to circumcise the toddler himself and had given the baby enough alcohol to poison him.

Veer, who was later castrated by Thériault, told a neighbor about the baby's death after he escaped the cult. Police raided the commune, arresting Thériault and the boy's parents. Veer was arrested a few days later in Quebec City. Ultimately, the prophet, parents, and babysitter were found criminally responsible in Samuel Giguère's death.

Shockingly, Thériault wasn't locked up long for the crime. But while he was behind bars, "Moses" made remorseful phone calls to his wives to assure them that the group would live together peacefully moving forward. After serving about two years in prison, Thériault was released and had the opportunity to make good on his promise. He reassembled the Ant Hill Kids and led them west to a 200-acre tract of land outside of Burnt River, Ontario.

But things were back to normal before too long, even with the increased scrutiny on the group by the authorities. The following year, when Lavallée's 5-month-old baby died at the commune, the coroner ruled that the death was due to sudden infant death syndrome. But Lavallée has said that the baby actually died after Thériault ordered the newborn to be wrapped in a blanket and put out in a wheelbarrow for hours in the dead of winter as a cruel (and deadly) punishment for crying.

In late 1985, Children's Aid Society, a government-approved child welfare agency, was tipped off that child abuse was happening at Thériault's commune. A raid led to 13 children being placed in foster care. The following year, an independent child abuse expert named Dr. Martine Miljkovitch evaluated eight of the children, aged three to nine, who had been removed from their parents at Burnt River. She heard unbelievable accounts that the children had assisted with births, watched adults have sex, and had sexual contact with each other. Miljkovitch recommended the children be allowed back in the care of

Thériault—who had been found criminally responsible in a toddler's death just three years earlier—and the Ant Hill Kids.

"There was a kind of naive attitude that you have to expose children to these things because they are part of nature. Certainly, the children were allowed to have sexual activities among themselves, but the principles behind it weren't bad," Miljkovitch said in a report. "Thériault would also demonstrate how the penis worked by masturbating in front of the children. But he didn't do it for his own satisfaction; he did it as a form of education. I thought that was an important distinction."

Luckily, Judge Lucien Beaulieu didn't take Miljkovitch's advice. Fearing for the safety of the children, Beaulieu made them wards of the crown and the children were placed with adoptive families.

"HE NEEDED TO SEE BLOOD"

On September 28, 1988, Thériault spent the morning drinking and picking fights. Suddenly, a calm came over him.

"He was a shark," Thériault's son Francois recalled in the *Whig* newspaper of his father's behavior that day. "He needed to see blood."

Before too long, Solange Boilard, 32, who had previously been complaining of stomach pains, was lying naked on a wooden bakery table. Thériault, the self-proclaimed savior who led the Israelites out of Egypt, wore red robes, jewelry, and a gold crown for the occasion. In this likely unsterile holy getup, while some of his own children looked on, he punched Boilard in the stomach and shoved an enema tube up her rectum to "treat" her with a combination of olive oil and molasses.

Then, sans anesthesia, Thériault cut open his spiritual wife's abdomen and ripped out a piece of her intestines using his bare (and presumably ungloved) hand. Once Thériault was done, he ordered Gabrielle Lavallée, his trusted nurse, to stitch her back up. Boilard died a day later and her body was buried on the Ant Hill Kids' property.

But Thériault didn't let her rest in peace. He was distraught that his beloved Solange, who served a somewhat powerful role as bookkeeper for the cult's bakery business, had died. He took her body to his altar, and then back to his bedroom to cuddle and tell her how much he loved her. She was buried in a pine coffin the following day, but Thériault, who was suicidal from the grief, ordered her dug up and cut a hole into her skull (according to Lavallée, this was so that he could masturbate into it). Boilard was buried and disinterred a number of times so that Thériault could perform more operations on her, including removing a part of her rib that he divided and gave to the other cult members to wear as a necklace.

Perhaps even more tragically, no one knew that Boilard had died until more than a year later.

ESCAPE FROM BURNT RIVER

Even though Lavallée could be trusted to do Theriault's medical bidding, she was often on the outs with Thériault and grouped among his less-favorite wives. This tension came to a breaking point in late summer 1989, when Thériault instructed his harem to write him letters that praised him as a leader. Lavallée couldn't bring herself to revere the man who controlled every aspect of her life, and who had disemboweled one of her spiritual sister-wives. To punish this act of insubordination, Thériault stabbed her hand to the kitchen table so that she couldn't leave and started slowly carving away at her arm for hours with the small blade of a carpet knife, down to the bone. Lavallée was pinned, completely unable to move, and already suffering from severed tendons. At a point she became completely numb and convinced that Thériault was finally going to kill her. In a moment of insight, Lavallée was enveloped by God's love and finally saw that Thériault wasn't a savior, but the devil. The devil later took her outside and amputated her arm with an axe, which was later crudely stitched up with twine and cauterized.

Lavallée waited nearly three weeks for the right moment to escape, and on August 14, 1989, fled through the woods and into the nearby town of Burnt River, clinging to life and weighing just 80 pounds when she emerged from the woods. Even then Lavallée stayed loyal to Thériault, and it was Thériault's legal wife, Gisèle, who confided in a welfare caseworker about the horrors endured at the commune. A few weeks later, police picked up Thériault on assault charges, as well as a few other cultists as accomplices. Thériault, who didn't know that the authorities knew anything about the Boilard killing, pleaded guilty to assaulting Lavallée. Nearly a year later, in December 1990, Thériault was finally slapped with second-degree murder charges for the disembowelment and killing.

Anticipating that Thériault's lawyer might try to have his client's murder charge bumped down to manslaughter because he was drunk during the incident, Constable Bob Bowen of the Ontario Provincial Police decided he needed to gather as much evidence as possible about additional crimes to have the cult leader deemed a dangerous offender by the courts. Bowen diligently interviewed Thériault's victims, collecting enough information and evidence to prove that the cult leader was responsible for at least 84 attacks. When this investigation came to light, Thériault's lawyer, Julian Falconer, cut a plea bargain for his client. Thériault pleaded guilty to second-degree murder, which means that the murder was not premeditated, under the stipulation that none of the other assaults were prosecuted. Because of this, most of Thériault's sordid behavior over the years never entered the public record. Thériault was sentenced to life in prison in 1993.

"REGRET IS TO NEVER BE ABLE TO DO IT AGAIN"

Thériault's life in prison consisted of writing poems, working on his art, and continuing to father children with three of his wives who stuck by their man. The first year that Thériault was behind bars, Francine Laflamme, 36, Chantal Labrie, 34, and Nicole Ruel, 35, moved into neighboring log cabins about half a mile away from Millhaven Institution, a maximum-security prison where Thériault was being held in Kingston, Ontario. The women ran a bakery and Francine waited her turn for a conjugal visit with Thériault, which rolled around about every six weeks, giving birth to her fifth child—his twenty-eighth—while he was behind bars.

Thirteen years into his sentence, Thériault came up before the parole board for the first time. Although Thériault had applied for parole, he asked the board not to release him from prison because he feared for his safety outside the penitentiary's gates. By this time, Thériault was being housed at Dorchester Penitentiary, a medium security prison in the Canadian province of New Brunswick. It wasn't up to Thériault whether he wanted to leave or not, as the parole board cited his drug and alcohol problems and deemed him a danger to society.

Lavallée was at the hearing.

"This man is very subtle, extremely manipulative. He's a psychopath. To me, to my eyes, he's a psychopath," she told *CBC News*. "You can see my face. I'm so glad. I'm really, really, really glad," Lavallée remarked, relieved that her ex-Messiah would remain behind bars. As for the wives, Lavallée said it was "very sad that those girls are still under his power."

In the end, Thériault had less to fear from the outside world than he did behind the barbed wire of Dorchester Penitentiary. On the morning of February 26, 2011, convicted murderer Matthew Gerrard MacDonald entered Thériault's cell and stabbed the former cult leader in the neck with a shank, killing him. According to the article "Canadian Messiah," apparently, MacDonald had a big problem with Thériault's treatment of women and children, and later confessed to prison guards that he had "sliced him up." The bloody end to Thériault's life was captured on closed-circuit video. He was 63 years old.

Following the fatal stabbing, Royal Canadian Mounted Police Sergeant Greg Lupson told the press that a 59-year-old inmate had been arrested in the incident and released back into general population pending charges. Three months later, MacDonald was charged with first-degree murder. He ended up pleading guilty to second-degree murder just days before his trial was set to start, and had an additional life term added on to his life sentence.

Three years before his demise, Thériault was back in the headlines when his artwork was discovered on a "murderabilia" website headquartered in the United States called murderauction.com. Unlike the Son of Sam laws in the US that make it difficult for criminals to profit from their crimes through book and TV deals and other ventures, Canada didn't have anything equivalent on the books. The following year, prison officials found a workaround, barring Thériault's poems and artwork from leaving the prison.

A quick search of murderauction.com at the time of writing shows that five pieces of Thériault memorabilia remain for sale, including a "rare hand tracing" listed for a starting bid of $100. A Polaroid of what appears to be cell bars signed "Roch Thériault" with an accompanying smiley face is active and can be yours for a minimum bid of $350. The highest-priced item that Thériault left behind was an abstract painting with two handprints, signed by "Roch Moises Thériault," which has a minimum asking bid of $9,500.

According to the auction site, Thériault was very private during his prison years and rarely corresponded with anyone outside of his family. It's possible to get a glimpse into one of

Canada's most notorious criminal mind through a brief poem that he wrote in 2011 that was available on the auction site in early 2018:

> *Le regret, c'est de ne plus jamais recommence*
> ("Regret is to never be able to do it again")

CHAPTER 5

DAVID KORESH AND THE BRANCH DAVIDIANS

Wayne Martin, a Harvard-educated lawyer, placed a 911 call to the McLennan County Sheriff's Department in Waco, Texas, on the morning of February 28, 1993. With the pops of gunfire in the background, Lieutenant Larry Lynch got on the line.

Lieutenant Larry Lynch, McLennan County Sheriff's Department: Hello, this is Lieutenant Lynch, can I help you?

Wayne Martin: Yeah, there's 75 men around our building shooting at us at Mount Carmel. Tell them there are women and children in here and to call it off!

Lieutenant Lynch: Hello? I hear gunfire. Oh, shit. Hello?

Wayne Martin: Call it off!

Lieutenant Lynch: Who is this? Hello? Hello? ... Oh my. Hello?

Martin stopped responding but kept the phone line open for the sheriff's lieutenant to hear screams and what sounded like automatic weapon fire on the 77-acre compound called Mount Carmel.

At one point the leader of this small, apocalyptic Christian group of Branch Davidians that called Mount Carmel home eventually got on the phone. David Koresh, who referred to himself as "the notorious" on the 911 call, was out of breath but much calmer than Martin.

"You brought a bunch of guys out here and you killed some of my children. We told you we wanted to talk. How come you guys, you ATF agents, try to be so big all the time?" Koresh seethed. "There is a bunch of us dead and a bunch of you guys dead. Now that's your fault ... We knew you were coming and everything."

The heavy gun battle between the Branch Davidians and the federal Bureau of Alcohol, Tobacco, Firearms and Explosives agents lasted about 45 minutes. By the time the clash was over, four ATF agents and six Branch Davidians were dead. But the standoff—which started as an effort to serve a search warrant for a suspected stockpile of weapons at Mount Carmel and to arrest Koresh on charges of unlawful possession of a destructive device—was far from over. The Branch Davidians refused to come out, which led to a 51-day standoff that quickly turned into a psychological cat-and-mouse game. Koresh gave long biblical teachings to the Federal Bureau of Investigation (FBI) hostage negotiation team and used children in the compound as bartering chips—he would agree to release one or two only after recordings of his teachings were played on the radio. FBI negotiators listened to Koresh's biblical musings and tried to steer conversations toward a surrender agreement for the cult leader and his roughly 100 followers. The government believed the Davidians had hundreds of weapons and a year's supply of food inside. After a few weeks, tactical teams upped the ante, cutting the power to Mount Carmel during that late Texas winter, shining spotlights inside, and playing loud and bizarre sounds, including dying rabbits, Christmas carols, Tibetan Buddhist chants, and Alice Cooper songs in hopes that sleep-deprivation tactics would eventually break down Koresh's followers.

But support was unwavering for Koresh, the 33-year-old high-school dropout and guitar enthusiast whom Davidians regarded as their prophet. Like many Christian offshoots that predict the end times, Koresh's sermons centered around the group going to heaven after a violent and final battle with the United States government. With the ATF shooting at their doorstep, Koresh seemed to have gotten it right.

And to his followers, Koresh was not only a biblical teacher, but the Lamb of God who knew the mysteries of the Book of Revelations and beyond. He wasn't necessarily a gifted orator but was quoted in the *Waco Tribune-Harald* as someone who could "make the scriptures come alive, harmonize them, and make them applicable in this day and age."

This allegiance led to a number of practices that were hard even for members in the group to justify, including Koresh having sexual relationships with teenage girls and taking more than a dozen women as his spiritual wives (and in some cases, snatching these women from their legal husbands).

Whether through Koresh's control or out of devotion to their leader, 82 Branch Davidians stayed with Koresh until the very end. On April 19, 1993—51 days after the gun battle—the government aggressively moved to end negotiations and flush the Branch Davidians out of their compound using tear gas and other tactical maneuvers. But the government's operation ended after a deadly inferno killed nearly everyone inside, and Waco became a rallying call about religious freedom and one's right to privacy, inspiring at least one terrorist attack on American soil.

HOW DAVID FOUND (AND LEAD) THE DAVIDIANS

The man who would become known around the world as David Koresh was born as Vernon Howell on August 17, 1959, in Houston, Texas. (For consistency, we'll refer to him as "Koresh" throughout, though the reader should note that he legally changed his name in 1990.) His mother, Bonnie Clark, came from a poor family and was just shy of 15 when he was born. Money was so tight that Bonnie had to work in the school cafeteria during lunch and clean bathrooms after school so that her family could afford to send her to a Seventh-day Adventist school. Clark met Koresh's father, Bobby Howell, when she was about 13, and Bonnie was kicked out of her religious school after being spotted kissing Howell in his pickup truck.

Koresh's father was absent from his early years, then completely out of the picture until around the time Koresh turned 19. As Koresh's mother wrote in her autobiography, Koresh was largely raised by his grandmother from ages two to four, and fell in love with Sabbath school as a little boy of four years old.

Koresh's mother remembers her son as a curious talker who always wanted to figure out how things worked, even as a little boy. She recalled, "all the women who ever met him—my sisters-in-law, mother-in-law, every female that ever met him—just fell in love with him. He was so cute and sweet."

Though media accounts would later describe Koresh as dyslexic, his mother claimed he was intelligent and had a different language disability. She also said he had many friends at school, countering a popular image in the media of Koresh as a loner, and that his teenage years revolved around playing guitar, listening to rock music, and fishing.

The future cult leader leaned upon his faith and his church during a period of heartbreak in his late teens. Koresh's first girlfriend, Linda, had gotten pregnant, and her father was so furious that he'd forbidden Koresh from seeing Linda or meeting the baby girl, whom she named Shea.

Koresh was baptized in the Seventh-day Adventist Church when he was 20 years old. You might recall the Seventh-day Adventists from Chapter 4 as the clean-living, apocalyptic church that Canadian cult leader Roch Thériault thrived in before being kicked out for his arrogant demeanor.

According to a 2014 Pew Research Center poll, Seventh-day Adventists are a small Christian group that make up 0.5 percent of the adult population in the United States (compared to 70.6 percent of the polled population that identified as Christian). They also ranked highest in racial and ethnic diversity, according to an analysis of the 2014 numbers, with 37 percent identifying as white, 32 percent as black, 15 percent as Latino, 8 percent as Asian, and 8 percent as other or mixed race.

This evangelical group grew out of nineteenth-century pastor William Miller's prediction that Jesus Christ would come back in 1844. Adventists, who sometimes refer to themselves as "God's peculiar people," believe that the Bible is the direct word of God and that Jesus will return to Earth sooner rather than later, observe the Sabbath on Saturday, and refrain from smoking and drinking. Many, but not all, are opposed to abortion and believe that humans did not evolve from primates, but instead have always existed in their current form.

Koresh, like Ant Hill Kids' leader Thériault, was initially seen as a rising star in the church. But Koresh was kicked out when his teachings radically deviated from the mainstream (and it probably didn't help that he had professed his love for his pastor's daughter). Shirley Burton from the Seventh-day Adventist Church world headquarters later told the *Chicago Tribune* that after two years, Koresh had been "disfellowshipped for bizarre beliefs and lifestyle," which included calling himself "Vernon Jezreel"—the avenging one—and teaching that Jesus is not the only person one can pray to for forgiveness.

When Koresh was about 22, he found his way to the Branch Davidians, an offshoot of the Seventh-day Adventists that was started in the late 1920s by Bulgarian immigrant Victor Houteff. Houteff started his own movement based on two concepts that mainstream church wasn't on board with: purifying the church from within and gathering 144,000 followers to survive the Second Coming. Houteff was the sole interpreter of the Bible, according to his teachings, and his successors would follow this lead. In the early years, Houteff's group was known as the Shepherd's Rod, and in 1935, Houteff and 37 of his followers settled about two miles outside of Waco and established a self-sufficient community that they named Mount Carmel.

According to the Texas State Historical Association, the group tried to stay as separate as possible from mainstream society to "avoid the corruptions of the world." The Branch Davidians farmed together and improved on their property, with some members working in nearby Waco to bring in extra money. Five years later, the Branch Davidians had nearly doubled in membership, and the Mount Carmel compound had 10 buildings and a sewage and telephone system.

Houteff died in 1955 and his wife, Florence, took over as the Branch Davidians' prophet. The group moved to a larger homestead about nine miles east of Waco, which they called the New Mount Carmel. It was there that 900 people from across the country gathered on Passover, 1959, to prepare for Jesus Christ's return, as Florence Houteff had predicted. Spoiler alert from the past: he didn't, and her incorrect prophecy led to a significant exodus of her followers.

During the 1960s there was a power struggle for the next prophet, and by the time Koresh showed up in the early 1980s, the Branch Davidians were led by Lois Roden, an older woman who had radically preached on the female character of the

Holy Spirit (she also taught that women should be ordained and published a journal on women's issues called *Shekinah*).

Roden was clearly taken with Koresh. Before long, Roden declared that Koresh was God's messenger, and he was preaching to the group. Though there were more than four decades between them, Roden and Koresh began a sexual relationship. One person who wasn't pleased with Roden grooming Koresh to become the Branch Davidians' next prophet was her adult son, George Roden, who'd assumed that he would be the next to lead the group.

Lois Roden's death in 1986 led to the inevitable power struggle between Koresh (who had married a 14-year-old named Rachel Jones two years earlier) and George Roden, who would later testify that Koresh had raped and brainwashed his mother. The younger Roden cast off Koresh and a group of his followers at gunpoint, and they set up camp in Palestine, Texas, living in shacks and crude abandoned structures that were by some accounts not much more than boxes.

Years later, after the government had cut power to the Branch Davidian compound during the 1993 standoff, Koresh's lieutenant Steve Schneider would recall the tenacity of the Branch Davidians who were used to no-frills living.

"That's one thing that doesn't bother these people," Schneider told FBI negotiators. "They don't care being without it. Because you've got to remember, they chose to, like me, originally in '87, to go over to Palestine, Texas, where all they had was lanterns, outdoor toilets, things of that nature ... No running water. So that way you find out if people are really honest in searching for truth. Or are they coming to live free and live off of someone else. So see, that's what that was all about. So number one, these people want eternal life."

Even with 100 miles between them, Koresh and Roden's feud continued. In 1987, Roden decided he was ready to settle the matter of the next rightful prophet once and for all and devised an appropriate challenge: a good old-fashioned resurrection. Roden went to the Mount Carmel cemetery and dug up the coffin of Anna Hughes, who had died back in 1968. Roden moved her coffin into the Branch Davidians' chapel, draping it with a Star of David flag, and tried (unsuccessfully) three times to revive the dead grandmother. Koresh never attempted this feat, but instead tried to gather evidence for authorities in hopes of getting Roden arrested on charges of corpse abuse.

In November 1987, Koresh led a group of his followers, clad in camouflage and brandishing assault-style weapons and a camera, to Mount Carmel. A gun battle ensued and Roden was shot, though not killed, and Koresh took back Mount Carmel by force.

Attempted murder charges were filed against Koresh and his followers, which led to an unusual trial that the *New York Times* described as a "circus." The most famous act happened one morning during the proceedings, when Koresh and other Branch Davidians carried Hughes's coffin up the steps of the McLennan County courthouse, hoping to have it admitted as evidence. (The judge didn't allow it, though the jury witnessed the spectacle, according to the *Washington Post*.) Media accounts say Koresh dressed up Hughes's skeleton with a pink bow for the occasion, though in her autobiography, Koresh's mother maintains Hughes had already been reburied by the time her coffin made it to the court.

An editorial that ran in the *Waco Tribune-Herald* called "the idea of a person's remains being disturbed for ritual's sake and then becoming a focus of a family feud is a sickening affront to this society's sense of decency," and called on the district attorney to look into charges against Koresh and his crew.

Jurors would later find several Branch Davidians not guilty, and a hung jury led to Koresh's acquittal (charges were later dropped). Charmed jurors would later be wined and dined by Koresh and the Davidians, who threw a party with nonalcoholic beer and vegetarian pizza to thank them for their civic duty.

Roden didn't get off so easily. Earlier that year, a US district judge had sentenced him to six months in prison after he filed multiple obscene legal appeals in his case to have Mount Carmel's land made tax-exempt, which included a call to God to "inflict AIDS, herpes, and the 'seven last plagues'" on judges. Less than a year after his release, Roden shot and killed Wayman Dale Adair, his 56-year-old roommate in Odessa. Roden later claimed that he shot Adair in self-defense because Koresh had sent him there to kill him. He was found not guilty by reason of insanity and committed to a state-run mental hospital in 1993.

Because the case against Koresh and his followers did not result in any convictions, the Branch Davidians' massive weapon and ammunition cache was returned to them as per Texas law.

In an article that ran in the days following the deadly ATF raid, *New York Times* reporter Adam Nossiter wrote that Koresh had indicated what they were capable of years earlier. "David Koresh and members of his insular religious sect gave the outside world a warning about his passionate attachment to firearms and his potential for violence. The outside world chose to look the other way."

THE HOUSE OF DAVID

With Roden out, Koresh was the undisputed leader of the Branch Davidians (no proof of resurrection power necessary). Over the next few years, about 150 people were living at Mount Carmel. More affluent members of the cult gifted properties and other high-priced items to the Davidians, including a $100,000 home in Pomona, California. Koresh split his time between California, where he often recruited young musicians like himself, and Mount Carmel, as well as taking trips to Australia, New Zealand, Canada, and England to proselytize.

Life for the Branch Davidians centered around Bible study and weapons training that would prepare the group for their remaining time on Earth before Christ came back. Days started with military-style exercises on an obstacle course. Every Branch Davidian, from very young children to the elderly, learned how to shoot a gun and was responsible for guarding the compound. According to ABC News, the Branch Davidian children were taught to chant: "We are soldiers in the army. We've got to fight. Some day we have to die. We have to hold up the blood-stained banner. We have to hold it up until we die." One former member told the *Waco Tribune-Herald* Branch

Davidians thought of themselves as "God's marines," because "if you can't die for God, you can't live for God."

Neighbors who lived near Mount Carmel often complained of the gunshots, which sounded as though they were being discharged from illegal automatic weapons. During a police visit to the compound, Branch Davidians said that they had put hell-fire switches on their guns, a legal modification to a semi-automatic gun's trigger system that makes it fire faster to mimic an automatic weapon.

It is important to note that until the ATF raid, the Branch Davidians seemed to have a good amount of interaction outside of Mount Carmel, with members holding jobs in the community such as lawyers, mail carriers, and auto mechanics. Whether or not Koresh's followers were truly allowed to leave during the 51-day siege, it appears that they were able to travel more freely in peaceful times than other cult leaders profiled in this book allowed.

Koresh was far from lenient in other areas, especially when it came to punishing the group's children, instructing women to beat their children until they bled using a wooden paddle for infractions as minor as spilled milk.

Like other cults, Koresh held marathon Bible study sessions, and like his Branch Davidian predecessors, Koresh was his followers' key to understanding biblical teachings. His teachings were often long and confusing, reinforcing the idea that their prophet needed to interpret the Bible for them. In *Cults in Our Midst*, sociologists Margaret Singer and Janja Lalich write that cults often use "speech filled with paradox and discrepancy" as a psychological persuasion technique during cult indoctrination. If the teaching is not logical, but is presented as so, it can "actually detach the listener from reality," they write.

Like many other millennialist religions, Koresh's focus was the Book of Revelations, in particular the seven seals teaching found in Revelation 6, which begins:

> Now I watched when the Lamb opened one of the seven seals, and I heard one of the four living creatures say with a voice like thunder, "Come!" And I looked, and behold, a white horse! And its rider had a bow, and a crown was given to him, and he came out conquering, and to conquer.

The seals are opened one by one, producing horses of different colors, bringing warfare, famine, pestilence, earthquakes. When the seventh and final seal was opened, everyone on Earth—even the most powerful kings—hid in caves and in between the rocks on mountains to hide from the wrath of the Lamb.

The Branch Davidians had long wondered who had the capability to open up the seven seals. But the identity of the Lamb wasn't clear to the Branch Davidians until 1989, when Koresh delivered his "New Light" teaching. According to Koresh, not only was he the Lamb from the Book of Revelations who held the key to open up the seven seals, but all the women in the cult now belonged to him. Koresh annulled all marriages (except for his own), instructing his male followers to practice celibacy and promising them that their perfect wives awaited them in heaven. Meanwhile, back on Earth, Koresh would tend to their former partners.

According to *New Yorker* staff writer Malcolm Gladwell, it made sense that Koresh was the Lamb: "That's why he was so good at making sense of the seven seals."

Koresh and Rachel Howell had their first child, named Israel, in 1985. Koresh's New Light teaching came the year after his first child outside his legal marriage, Sky Borne Okimoto, was born. Not all Branch Davidians were on board with Koresh disbanding their marriages, then segregating the sexes during practically every activity but Bible study. Some members left the church following this decree. Longtime member Clive Doyle, who survived the Waco siege, recalled wondering "is this God or is this horny old David talking?"

Another woman remembered the prophecy a different way. "He was supposed to be the son of God," she told the *Waco Tribune-Herald*. "He said God was really lonesome, and he wanted grandchildren. It was like the Scriptures kind of said it, but they didn't really. It was like he was giving God grandchildren."

Whether God or just horny old David, Koresh got to work assembling his harem, which he called the "House of David." His spiritual wives were given coveted Star of David pendants to wear on necklaces. More women from Mount Carmel started giving birth to children and leaving the father's name on the birth certificate blank, a tactic used by Koresh to keep a low profile as to the number of his offspring, which had swelled to at least 15 by 1993. More disturbing—and criminal—was the young age of his spiritual wives. Koresh reportedly married the 12-year-old sister of his legal wife, Rachel. Cult child Kiri Jewell, then 14, testified in 1995 that Koresh had sex with her in a motel room when she was just 10 years old. And this wasn't the first time that Koresh was allowed to be alone with Jewell. Koresh had taken her on a motorcycle trip with some of the guys to California's Mount Baldy when she was just 7. Koresh took the child for a ride on a chairlift, and over the snowless ski trails, told her that she'd be one of his wives someday, too.

Kiri's mother, Sherri Jewell, was one of Koresh's spiritual wives as well, and Kiri recalled that it wasn't out of the ordinary for Koresh to sleep in a bed with women and children. "Sometimes I fell asleep in his room after a meeting or maybe I'd fall asleep on his bed watching MTV. I didn't even think about it, because the women and girls were all David's wives, or would be, and many of the kids were his, too."

Robyn Bunds, a former spiritual wife who left the group after having a son with Koresh, described a less egalitarian vibe among the House of David insiders. "It was like a beauty contest ... all of us battling against each other to be the woman that God thinks is the greatest," Bunds told the *Waco Tribune-Herald*. Even among mother and daughter: Bund's mother, Jeannine, was also in the House of David.

SINFUL MESSIAH?

In 1989, a group of concerned Branch Davidians, which included Koresh's ex-chief lieutenant Marc Breault, broke away from the group and moved to Australia. The following year, their lobbying led Australian authorities to investigate Koresh for child abuse and weapons violations. But even with the help of a hired private investigator, Breault's group was unable to convince American authorities on local, state, and federal levels that Koresh was a threat to his followers without direct evidence.

Breault, an American, and other Australian Branch Davidians returned to the United States in 1992 to testify in the Kiri Jewell child custody case after her father, a disc jockey who lived in Michigan who was not a Branch Davidian, sued for custody. The judge ultimately ordered Koresh to stay away from Jewell.

Letters in a Koresh FBI file released through a Freedom of Information Act request show that the agency started investigating tips into weapons at the Branch Davidian compound in 1992. Authorities also received letters alleging servitude, slavery, and child abuse at Koresh's compound, as well as plans for a mass suicide. After both unannounced and announced visits, Child Protective Services closed their investigation and US attorneys did not have evidence to prosecute Koresh for the other claims.

But the ATF continued looking into the accounts that Koresh and the Branch Davidians were manufacturing weapons at the compound. ATF started planning to serve a search warrant on the rural complex and decided to use a dynamic entry with flash-bang grenades and agents swarming the building from the roof and windows, even though most of the men in the group would be away at work during the raid's anticipated 10 a.m. start time.

In February 1993, letters continued to be sent to Congress members in Texas and Michigan warning authorities that children were being abused at Mount Carmel, as well as information that the Branch Davidians were planning a mass suicide for Passover that spring. That month, the local *Waco Tribune-Herald* published a series of stories called "Sinful Messiah." Over eight months, reporters Darlene McCormick and Mark England interviewed former Branch Davidians, and the series exposed the claims of sex abuse and Koresh's numerous wives living on Waco's outskirts.

In late February, a US judge signed off on a search and arrest warrant that would permit ATF to search the Branch Davidian compound and arrest Koresh on charges of possessing illegal automatic machine guns.

"WE KNEW YOU WERE COMING"

It was a cold and rainy Sunday morning. The helicopters started circling Mount Carmel around 9:55 a.m. on February 28, 1993. Then, two cattle trailers pulled up and approximately 100 agents ran out, throwing grenades, putting up ladders, climbing up the building, and demanding that everyone inside come out.

It's unclear who fired the first shots. After the dust settled, both sides would allege the other fired first. But one thing was certain: David Koresh and the Branch Davidians were not caught off guard.

Koresh had been tipped off, it turned out, after a television cameraman also working on a scoop stopped to ask a postal worker if he knew how to get to Mount Carmel. The mailman happened to be a Branch Davidian and raced back to tell Koresh what was going to happen.

ATF agent Roland Ballesteros would later recall running to the front door yelling "Police, search warrant!" and seeing Koresh standing there. He backed up and shut the door. "And before long," Ballesteros told ABC News, "It was like everybody starts shooting at once. You couldn't hear anything."

As bullets flew through the walls and windows, Branch Davidian mothers grabbed their children to shield them from the assault, taking cover under beds. Several Branch Davidians recall that Koresh had instructed everyone to return to their rooms before the shooting started. The Branch Davidians and ATF agents fired for about 45 minutes, followed by more infrequent exchanges of gunfire. Four ATF agents were killed, along with six Branch Davidians. A seventh cult member would be shot and killed later that evening after he returned home from his job at an auto repair shop and tried to get in the house by breaking through the police barricade. His body would lie there for five days until the FBI permitted Branch Davidians to move and bury him. Koresh suffered a bullet wound to his abdomen that would go untreated for the next 51 days, as the leader and many of his followers remained in their compound despite law enforcement's exhaustive efforts to coax them out.

By the end of that day, more than 60 reporters had gathered on a ridge a few miles away from Mount Carmel, and the story of David Koresh and his group of followers became international news. The following morning, the FBI took over as head of the operation, which involved hundreds of law enforcement officers from multiple agencies that included US Customs and Border Protection, McLennan County Sheriff, Texas Rangers, Texas Department of Public Safety, US Army, and Texas National Guard.

THE STANDOFF

Neither Koresh nor his followers planned on coming out of Mount Carmel anytime soon. The FBI brought in a team of hostage negotiators and opened up a line of communication between the compound and the law-enforcement officers. Koresh, his second-in-command Steve Schneider, and other Branch Davidians often spent hours a day on the phone with the negotiators, discussing logistics such as having milk for the children delivered along with legal documents and arranging for the fallen Branch Davidians to be buried. Koresh talked for hours about scriptures, delivering sermons and testing the Biblical knowledge of the FBI team.

In the first five days, Koresh and the negotiators arranged for 21 children to leave the compound. After that, children were released periodically, and Heather Jones became the last child to leave the compound (though many children remained inside) on March 5. The Branch Davidian children ranged in age from 13 months to 13 years old and were taken to the Methodist Children's Home. Caretakers said the children were bright, though sheltered, and were unfamiliar with modern conveniences such as baths and flush toilets. Psychiatrist Bruce Perry said at least half of the children had seen a dead body, and most of the children had seen blood, and that it took two weeks to get their heart rates to return to an average level.

"Their whole world was completely shattered. They were in the care of people whom they didn't trust. And they had no idea what was going to happen," Perry told ABC News. The children spent two months at the home, attending school, therapy, and getting time to play like children (and no military drills). After the standoff ended, the children were either placed with foster families or back with their own parents if the adult Branch Davidian could prove they had firm ties to reality.

Koresh viewed the ATF raid as a religious attack, not a law-enforcement effort to execute a search warrant. Early in the negotiations, Koresh and his followers worked with the FBI to organize a national radio broadcast so that Koresh could share his important message, with the understanding that Koresh would surrender after his teachings were played. On March 1, Koresh agreed that he and his followers would come out after his message was broadcast, and on March 2, an hour-long tape of Koresh's teachings was played on the Dallas radio station KRLD. Three prison buses, as well as ambulances, were moved close to the compound in anticipation of the release. The Branch Davidians informed them that Koresh was being moved down the stairs on a stretcher because of his gunshot wounds. But then Koresh decided to have an impromptu prayer session, which led to a message from God that Koresh and his followers should remain inside. The FBI would have to wait.

Earlier in the negotiations, FBI negotiators sent a videotape into the compound as a way to introduce themselves and make them appear more human to Koresh and his followers. On March 8, the Davidians sent back a tape of David Koresh introducing his children and inviting them to wave to the camera. In it, Koresh rocks a smiling toddler named Bobby on his lap, plays with the baby's hair, and talks about the values that are important to his group.

"This is my family, and no one is going to come in on top of my family and start pushing my family around. It's just not going to happen, ain't going to happen," Koresh says. "You come pointing guns in the direction of my wife and my kids and damn it, I'll meet you at the door, anytime." No one would see this tape until months after the siege was over because the FBI was concerned that Koresh would gain sympathy, according to a Department of Justice report, and the video wasn't publicly released until after the fire.

While Koresh was working to convince negotiators that he was a godly family man, law enforcement was concerned that he was orchestrating a mass suicide. Memos dated March 8 and 9 portray Koresh as a delusional fanatic and conman who purposely attacked the ATF agents to set off a series of events to fulfill his religious teachings on the apocalypse. Experts believed that Koresh would rather die than lose his standing in his group as the Messiah, and recommended turning up the pressure by shutting off utilities, moving equipment, and periodically jamming radio or stopping negotiations as a way to "break Koresh's spirit because his psychopathic tendencies to control and manipulate have caused the negotiations to meet with limited success."

Members of the FBI negotiation team would later claim that this aggressive approach harmed their progress. Some of these tactics, such as shutting off the power on cold winter nights and using floodlights for sleep deprivation, were adding more stress, chaos, and anger to the Branch Davidians, who had to ration their water, survive on two ready-to-eat meals a day, and use kerosene lanterns for light and buckets for toilets. Some of the adults who left the compound were slapped with conspiracy to commit murder and other serious charges, making it unlikely that other members would willingly come out. During the 51 days, Branch Davidians held up handwritten banners in their windows with messages such as "We want our phone fixed," "God help us, we want the press," and "Rodney King we understand," the latter referring to the black taxi driver beaten by police officers in 1991, an event that led to riots. King famously declared, "Can't we all just get along?"

Over four weeks, negotiations led to 35 people coming out, 21 of them children.

After Koresh failed to come out in early March, his lawyer told the FBI that the group was planning to surrender after they observed Passover, which was expected to take place around April 6. While the government was busy demanding that large numbers of Davidians come out and bulldozing fences and other property when they didn't, two religious scholars named Phillip Arnold and James D. Tabor appeared on a Dallas morning talk show, KGBS, appealing to Koresh to get to work outlining his prophecy on the seven seals. (KGBS host Ron Engelman had already expressed his negative opinions of the ATF raid and FBI standoff.)

"The idea was that we are religious scholars who might give him a sympathetic hearing instead of just saying he was a nut," Tabor said in an interview with the *Waco Tribune-Herald.* "We didn't just say, 'This is crazy.' That wasn't part of our strategy."

While Tabor and Arnold disagreed with Koresh's biblical interpretation, they had spoken with Livingstone Fagan, who had left the compound on March 22 and relayed Koresh's teaching that they were living during the time of the fifth seal, which predicts two rounds of violence. The ATF raid was the first. The Davidians were waiting on a second, the scholars realized. "So far, just snippets and rumors have come out about his message. Now he sees a chance for more. What does every prophet want? A hearing. We feel this is a positive step. Hopefully, he won't feel so backed into a corner. We want them to come out," Tabor added in that interview.

By mid-April, Koresh was hard at work on his manuscript. It took him about a day and a half to finish his writing on the first seal, and he told FBI negotiators that he would plan to come out after he finished his work. Government officials estimated that it would take Koresh another two weeks, and while the Lamb was fervently writing, Attorney General Janet Reno, who had been sworn in after the raid had started, reviewed plans to flush the Davidians out using CS tear gas. Reno, according to a government report, wanted to see additional information, including the effect of tear gas on children and pregnant women. On April 17, she approved a plan after being assured that the tear gas wouldn't have any fatal or lasting effects on the youngest of Koresh's followers. Reno briefed President Bill Clinton the following day, and outside of Waco, armored vehicles started clearing the Branch Davidians' vehicles, including Koresh's prized Chevy Camaro, to make way for the operation. Inside the compound, Davidians held their children up to the window and unfurled a sign with an ominous Bible verse from the Old Testament Book of Isaiah: "Flames Await."

YOU HAVE HAD YOUR 15 MINUTES OF FAME

"Nothing about April 19 started out normal, nothing," Branch Davidian David Thibodeau told ABC News. High winds approached 35 miles an hour. There was no routine 5 a.m. shift change.

Then, shortly before 6 a.m., FBI Chief Negotiator Byron Sage called the compound, telling Schneider to expect the tear gas as armored vehicles advanced and took their positions around the building. The Davidians tossed out their phone, and the FBI started delivering their message over a loudspeaker system instead:

> *We will continue to introduce tear gas into the building in an effort to direct you out of the building. This is not an assault. You are not to come out of that building with any type of weapon or anything that would appear to be a firearm.*
>
> *We do not intend to enter your building at this time. This is not an assault. Do not fire your weapons. Do not appear at the windows with anything that could be construed as being a weapon. If you fire, your fire will be returned. Do not shoot. This is not an assault.*

Then Sage started addressing Koresh, whom he had gotten to know through their many phone calls during the standoff:

> *You need to realize that this standoff is over. It is now time to exit the compound in an orderly fashion ... The time is now, David. It's time to come out of that compound. You've stressed the fact that you have concern for your followers.*

You've stressed the fact that you are still working on the seven seals. Demonstrate your concern for your followers, we will demonstrate our ability in allowing you to continue to work on the seven seals following your release ... This standoff, David, is over. The delay is over. It is time to move forward and get this matter resolved. We've been here for over 50 days. We will not be here any longer.

You claim to be the prophet. You claim to be the Messiah. The time to lead your people out is now.

But no one came out, and armored vehicles started shooting tear gas canisters into Mount Carmel. Inside, the adults put on gas masks and children, who were too small to fit into their own, were given wet rags to cover their faces. Half an hour in, the whole building had been tear gassed, but the FBI continued gassing the building for three and a half more hours. At one point, the FBI ran out of CS gas and had to wait for a backup supply to come in from Houston. Some 400 rounds were used that day. After 9 a.m., the armored vehicles started bashing into the building's walls to make an escape route for the Branch Davidians, and snipers were deployed. All the while, Koresh and his followers fired on approaching vehicles, and women and children took cover in an underground bunker, supposedly reading their Bibles and listening to the radio.

The flames were first spotted shortly after noon and moved so fast that the building was completely engulfed in flames. Nine Branch Davidians escaped—no one bringing a child or a dog, Sage would later remark in the documentary *Waco, Madman or Messiah?*. Survivor Clive Doyle recalled the heat of the fire caused his skin to roll off his hands, his jacket to melt into his body. Ruth Riddle, another survivor, escaped the flames with a disk of Koresh's writings on the seven seals in the pocket of her fatigue pants. (Since the power had been cut, Koresh and his followers used a car battery to power his computer.) Other survivors lost their fingers and endured numerous operations on their extensive burns.

But most of the Davidians did not make it out alive; 73 people died that day, 23 of them children. Not all the remains were identifiable, though autopsies would later find that many people, children included, were killed by bullets. At least one toddler was stabbed to death.

Fagan, who had helped explain Koresh's teachings to the religious scholars, recalls watching the fire on television in his jail cell, and the pride that he felt in the followers refusing to come out of the flames—even his mother and wife, who perished. "Dying was the right thing to do," Kat Schroeder, who left during the standoff, recalled in the documentary, "I should have died too."

Most of the surviving Branch Davidians maintained the fire started because of the government assault. Some experts, including sociology professor Stuart A. Wright, have written that the high quantities of CS used in the FBI's attack could have started the fire, and that it's possible that the lanterns that the group was using for light tipped over and ignited the blaze.

But survivor Graeme Craddock maintains that he saw someone pouring what appeared to be fuel on the floor and hearing an order to start the fire. The official arson report concluded that the fire had been intentionally set inside the building at three different points as a way for Koresh to orchestrate his death and the death of his followers. Infrared cameras, as well as recordings captured from the bugged building, indicated that the fire started within the compound, not from the tear gas. Attorney Edward S.G. Dennis would later conclude in his report for the Department of Justice that "the stand-off was a mass suicide choreographed by Koresh over a two-month period."

AFTERMATH

Mount Carmel was already a scene before the fire ended the siege. Reporters acted as if they were away at summer camp, playing cards and shooting the shit on lawn chairs outside of their trailers. Protesters showed up to condemn the ATF, including future Oklahoma City bomber Timothy McVeigh, who sold pro-gun bumper stickers out of his car. Two years later, McVeigh, with Terry Nichols and two other accomplices, detonated a homemade bomb outside the Alfred P. Murrah Federal Building in Oklahoma City, killing 168 people and wounding nearly 700 people on the second anniversary of the Waco fire.

Waco and Mount Carmel became tourist destinations as well that summer, with T-shirt vendors and overseas visitors coming to see the site that many in Waco city government would like the world to forget about. That October, a "prophetic rock requiem and memorial concert" was held to raise money for a memorial marker for the Branch Davidians and ATF agents. Eli Worden and the Free Spirit Band played a song called "From the Ashes," which Worden told the *Waco Tribune-Herald* was a

Christian tune inspired by a dream he had years earlier that mirrored the siege.

Though the ATF raid and FBI standoff were highly criticized as a militarized aggression, government officials maintained that the agencies delivered a justifiable response to federal agents being shot and killed. That September, a damning report by the Treasury Department, the government branch agency that oversees the ATF, revealed that officials had altered documents to cover up that they went ahead with serving the search warrant even though Koresh had been tipped off. ATF Director Stephen Higgins and other high-ranking officials stepped down.

The following February, 11 Branch Davidians were acquitted of the top charges against them, including murder and conspiracy to commit murder, in a six-week criminal trial held in San Antonio. Four Branch Davidians were cleared, and the remaining received prison sentences for charges such as aiding and abetting in voluntary manslaughter and weapons charges. Prosecutors were unable to prove that the specific Davidians on trial fired the shots that killed the four ATF agents. Defense attorneys questioned the use of force against the group by "overgrown GIs," and brought up the Treasury Department's damning findings. The *New York Times* reported that the verdict led to "jubilation among the defense lawyers and a stone-faced reaction from prosecutors." Nonetheless, Attorney General Reno released a statement that the jury had sent a message that the killing of the ATF agents was not "justified … [and] the shooting of law-enforcement officers doing their duty can never be tolerated."

The trial never managed to answer the biggest question—who fired first?—despite the ATF's previous claims that they had a video recording of the raid. The ATF had mounted a camera to a telephone pole near Mount Carmel's entrance to capture the raid, but later said that the tape was blank.

That fall, five Branch Davidians were sentenced to 40 years in prison for their involvement in the ATF shootout, though the jury and defense had asked for leniency. Judge Walter S. Smith said he was bound by federal sentencing guidelines. The Supreme Court later reduced their sentences to about 13 years, and all have since been released from prison.

Multiple civil lawsuits would be filed in the coming years. In 2000, the government dismissed a wrongful death lawsuit filed by the Branch Davidians, ensuring that federal agents could not be held liable for the deaths at Mount Carmel. Several ATF agents sued the *Waco Tribune-Herald*, KWTX-TV, and American Medical, an ambulance company whose driver had tipped off the press, alleging that the media was to blame for the shootout. The case was settled for an undisclosed amount in October 1996 with the media companies not accepting responsibility for any wrongdoing.

On the eve of the fifth anniversary of the Waco fire in 1998, Clive Doyle, who had been released after spending five years in prison, was gearing up to open a small museum at Mount Carmel that would include a timeline of events and videos of Koresh's sermons. Crape myrtles and crosses had been laid for each of the victims. The property, which still listed Koresh on the deed, was also the site of a turf war against a rival faction headed by a familiar name: (Amo Bishop) Roden. The museum stayed open until Doyle packed up and moved back to Waco in 2006.

In a 2004 auction, Koresh's beloved '68 Camaro, with "DAVID'S 427 GO GOD" engraved on the engine, fetched a measly $37,000—much less than anticipated for this grim collector's item.

By the twentieth anniversary in 2013, the Branch Davidians were led by Charles Pace. (Three years later, as the country geared up for the 2016 presidential election, Pace claimed that Hillary Rodham Clinton was behind the siege and that Trump and Koresh would have been allies.) Davidian survivors continue to hold their annual reunion, which draws about 50 people, in Waco, not Mount Carmel. ATF has a private memorial, and the city, which has long worked to distance itself from the tragedy, did not have any sort of public recognition.

"There was a feeling that it's one of those things that's probably best left alone," McLennan County Historical Commission Chairman Van Messirer told the *Waco Tribune-Herald*.

CHAPTER 6

ORDER OF THE SOLAR TEMPLE

They were business executives for luxury watch brands, doctors, mayors of Canadian cities, journalists, government administrators, and Olympians (perhaps even the Princess of Monaco was one of them)—the type of people you might expect to find spending their weekend in the Alps. But unlike their upper-crust counterparts who sipped Scotch *après-ski*, these men and women donned silk robes and participated in secret rituals inside chalets in remote, snowy corners of Switzerland and Canada.

The Order of the Solar Temple was started in 1984 by Joseph Di Mambro, a homeopathic doctor and a jeweler-turned-professional mystic. Members believed that they were part of an unbroken lineage dating back to the Knights Templar of the Middle Ages. This elite fighting squad protected Christendom during the Crusades and, once the enthusiasm for holy wars had waned, became a cadre of powerful bankers. The original order is believed to have died out when dozens of members were accused of heresy and burned at the stake in the early 1300s.

Like their medieval counterparts, the Order of the Solar Temple engaged in top-secret initiations, as well as other rituals that involved prayers, swords, and endless glasses of champagne. As the twentieth century came to a close, 74 members of the Order of the Solar Temple would meet a fiery demise as intentionally set fires ripped through their swanky digs, burning many cultists so badly that coroners had to use dental records to identify their bodies. When the embers had cooled and investigators got to work, the group's intentions wouldn't become much clearer—especially when it became apparent that many of the cultists had died from bullet wounds to the head that were not self-inflicted. Was this mass suicide? Mass murder? Or were these victims casualties of a worldwide money-laundering and gun-running scheme? And, if so, what about the letters, mailed out to newspapers and government officials, that described their deaths as a transit to the "Dog Star" Sirius?

FROM THE KNIGHTS TEMPLAR TO THE ORDER OF THE SOLAR TEMPLE

Joseph Di Mambro, the Order of the Solar Temple's "dictator," was born in Pont-Saint-Esprit, France, in 1924. Other than his professional training as a jeweler and watchmaker, not much else is known about Di Mambro's life before the 1950s. During that decade, Di Mambro joined the Rosicrucian Order, a mystical secret society influenced by a German doctor named Christian Rosenkrauz (though many scholars believe he never actually existed) that was heavily recruiting in France to combat dwindling membership numbers. Di Mambro remained a member of the neo-Templar group until 1969, which also taught ideas from New Age, Catholic, and theosophy (a mix of Buddhism, Hinduism, and scientific inquiry) traditions.

The original Knights Templar was started as a Catholic monastic organization by Hugues de Payens around the year 1118. The knights dressed in long white robes embellished with red crosses and were initially tasked with protecting Christian pilgrims traveling to the Holy Land from highway robbers. This scrappy startup played up their impoverished status and selfless motivations, calling themselves the "Poor Knights of Christ" in the early years. About 20 years after forming, the Knights Templar received official endorsement from the Catholic Church and quickly started amassing wealth from donors who admired their front-line bravery (even though only about 10 percent of members who took the top-secret oath were actually soldiers). Beyond the battlefield, the Knights Templar started lending money, establishing early forms of banking in Europe (while enjoying a tax-free status). With the ability to bypass local laws, they were incredibly powerful, answering only to the pope.

By the early 1300s, Jerusalem and other Holy Land strongholds had fallen under Ottoman control, and dueling monastic orders were making things difficult for both Philip IV of France (who also owed quite a bit of money to the Knights Templar banks) and Pope Clement V. The beginning of the end for the original order came on Friday, October 13, 1307, when Philip ordered a group of knights arrested and charged with several offenses, including heresy, fraud, and sodomy. Three years later, 54 knights were burned at the stake, effectively wiping out the order. Although rumors were passed down through French and German groups that the knights had secretly survived, most modern scholars have found this notion to be nothing more than romanticized rumors. The neo-Templar movement emerged in France following the French Revolution, and many modern groups trace their lineage back to l'Ordre du Temple, which was started in the early 1800s by Bernard-Raymond Fabré-Palaprat.

Like many cult leaders, Di Mambro dabbled in different religious orders before gaining the clout and confidence necessary for him to branch out on his own. Perhaps the greatest influence on the Order of the Solar Temple was Jacques Breyer, a French author who is credited with a modern resurgence of the Templar order in the 1950s, and in particular his idea of the doctrine of soul travel between life on Earth and eternal existence.

After a short stint in a French jail for practicing psychology without a license, Di Mambro opened up the Center for Preparing the New Age in 1973 and became a full-time spiritual leader three years later. Di Mambro led this group, which was also known as the Golden Way, in simple rituals and encouraged them to give up their money and possessions. By emphasizing frugality, Di Mambro was able to acquire a comfortable home in Geneva for his followers. He would later be remembered as a mix of a fraud and true believer, a father-like figure who could get away with being very controlling because of the love and devotion of his followers, who craved his attention.

As Di Mambro was growing a financial base, a handsome young doctor 20 years his junior was having a spiritual awakening in the Philippines. Luc Jouret, born in the Belgian Congo (now Zaire) in 1947, had studied medicine at the Free University of Brussels and spent several years as a surgeon. In the East, Jouret became interested in alternative and holistic forms of medicine, and started practicing homeopathy, which uses plants, minerals, and other natural ingredients to address diseases and other ailments. Jouret also drew upon meditation and macrobiotics as a way to help cure his patients from the inside out, and established a practice in Leglise, Belgium, in 1981. Jouret was accomplished, charismatic, athletic, and charming—everything Di Mambro knew that he himself was not and what a religious leader should be.

Jouret, who had ties to communist groups during his teenage and university years, had shifted his interest toward the occult. By the early 1980s, Jouret was a rising star in the Renewed Order of the Temple, a group started by an aging former Gestapo agent named Julien Origas (many other neo-Templar groups had far-right leanings as well). Di Mambro and Jouret first met around this time, with Di Mambro recognizing the young doctor's talents for public speaking. It's possible that Di Mambro was the one who introduced Jouret to Origas in an effort to gain control of the Renewed Order.

By 1983, Jouret had moved up to the rank of grand master in the Renewed Order. But according to Origas's widow,

Genevieve Origas, other members of the group eventually kicked Jouret out.

"He was a smooth talker, and he drew people to him," Genevieve Origas told *Newsweek* after the first wave of murder-suicides in 1994. "But he began to develop ideas we didn't like. Plus, his main aim was to get money and girls."

With Jouret out of the Renewed Order of the Temple, he and Di Mambro teamed up to start the Order of the Solar Temple in 1984. Jouret was the charismatic, public face and main recruiter of the organization, while Di Mambro was the more appealing leader to insiders, the behind-the-scenes master and representative for the Mother Lodge in Zurich, where 33 elder masters supposedly made up the innermost circle of the organization.

"For members of the group, the real charismatic personality was Jo Di Mambro," said religious scholar Jean-Francois Mayer during a 1998 conference on apocalyptic cults. "He wasn't an eloquent speaker. But when I spoke with former members, and I told them that, they were just incredulous. Jo Di Mambro, they would say, he was brilliant, he was extraordinary, and so on, because those people invested him with the qualities of a cosmic master."

Potential members were introduced to Jouret through either a public forum or one of the motivational speeches he was hired to give to companies on topics such as being happy at work and developing self-awareness. Training programs have long been a way for cults to recruit new followers, claiming to increase worker productivity, while in fact, they might cause more harm if thought-reform techniques are used on employees.

In the late 1980s, Hydro-Quebec, the public Canadian electric company, hired Jouret to give two motivational talks to employees. During this time, he supposedly galvanized 20 staffers to join the Order of the Solar Temple. The cult's next level was the Amanta or Archedia clubs, and the final level was the International Chivalric Organization of the Solar Tradition, a secret and elite group that members had to be initiated into as they pledged their allegiance to Jouret and Di Mambro (along with making significant financial contributions). Membership numbers peaked at around 500. The group appealed almost exclusively to "disaffected Catholics" from countries in French-speaking Europe, as well as Canada and Martinique, a French territory in the Caribbean.

Like many cults, the Order of the Solar Temple didn't reveal their secret knowledge of the workings of the universe to just anyone. In fact, the innermost circle of members was so secretive that Olympian skier-turned-businessman Jean Vuarnet had no idea that his wife and son were members until they were questioned by the police after the 1994 fires. And it wasn't until Jean's son, Patrick Vuarnet, reached the "golden circle" that he learned his mother, Edith, was also a high-ranking cultist. (Patrick and Edith Vuarnet died in a later cult fire.)

Central to Solar Temple beliefs was the idea that the apocalypse was imminent, and all the signs were in front of our eyes—holes in the ozone layer, the AIDS crisis, endless ethnic conflicts. "The present world chaos is not just by chance," Jouret once remarked at a lecture. As the group developed, and splits in leadership and credibility emerged, so did an idea that there was a way to escape this destruction. Those who had woken up to the Solar Temple's teachings could use their deaths as a gateway to a higher consciousness and be transported to the star Sirius, where they would live on as luminous, celestial beings.

While few actually became members of the Order of the Solar Temple's secret inner circle, these apocalyptic teachings were made available to anyone who attended one of Jouret's public lectures. Mayer, who also worked as an analyst for the Swiss government during the 1990s, said that he attended a Jouret talk billed as "Love and Biology" in 1987. But after the first 10 or 20 minutes, Jouret started explaining to the audience that "volcanoes are about to erupt, forests are dying, this Earth can no more endure those atrocities generated by mankind, and so on." These, according to Mayer, were typical talking points for a Jouret speaking event.

Another central ideological thread was that nothing was left to chance. No one casually attended a Solar Temple lecture; they had been reincarnated specifically to join the group. And those lucky enough to be inducted into the Solar Temple were told that they were otherworldly noble travelers who transcended time and space and were born on Earth to perform a specific mission.

According to Hermann Delorme, who left the organization after a run-in with Canadian authorities in 1993, he became so "disengaged and disconnected" from the outside world that nothing mattered to him but the Order of the Solar Temple.

"It flatters your ego to be part of a group that designs itself as the elite, that are the chosen ones, how can you not feel good about it?" Delorme said in a documentary, *The Order of the Solar Temple*. "I actually believed that I was superior to most other people on this planet, that I had been chosen, and I would start considering other people as being less than I was—not aware, not awake, having no idea of what life was actually all about, so there was no other option for me than to stay within the group ... that's where my salvation was," said Delorme, adding that he would have done anything to stay with Jouret and have a chance to be in contact with extraterrestrials.

Solar Temple cult rituals often started with a confession or guided meditation that instructed members to imagine light particles flowing in and out of their bodies. Ceremonies included prayers and readings from the Gospel of John and the esoteric writer Alice Bailey. According to some former members, there were less pious traditions as well, such as members being instructed to wear plastic bags over their heads to remind them of the disconnect between human and nature. Drugs were also supposedly used before rituals, disguised in soup or coffee, so that cult members might engage in activity that their sober selves would not allow, such as signing over their assets. As often seen in cults, Di Mambro was involved in approving or denying marriages in the cult, and even decided who would have children and what their babies would be named. With the exception of a group that traveled to Quebec to start a farm, many Order of the Solar Temple members did not live communally and held down jobs and homes outside of the group.

Around 1986, about a dozen Europeans who had followed Jouret and Di Mambro to Canada established an organic farm at the site of a former Catholic monastery in Sainte-Anne-de-la-Pérade, a small town of about 2,000, best known as a prime ice fishing location. The commune was viewed as a place for the group to buckle down and survive the impending apocalypse. Rose-Marie Klaus, who would become a vocal opponent of the cult in the following decade, claimed in a Radio Canada interview that her then-husband gave Solar Temple leaders $500,000 to get the farm going.

In Quebec, Jouret became more obsessed with apocalyptic thought, as well as the imminent threat of nuclear or environmental destruction. These end-time musings supposedly led to a split in the group, though it should be noted that Di Mambro was also very concerned with the future of the planet: Papers were later found indicating the Order of the Solar Temple's assets should be left to environmental groups, and Di Mambro reportedly kept with him a portable device to measure air quality.

SLOUCHING TOWARD TRANSIT

By the early 1990s, cracks began to emerge in the Solar Temple. Wealthy members who had donated millions of Swiss francs to the group wanted to know in detail how their money was being spent. (A search of Di Mambro's mansion after his death found that the man who encouraged his followers to eschew material goods himself possessed four red Ferraris and a Lamborghini, and Di Mambro and Jouret co-owned at least 60 properties on three continents.) The influential French government—backed anti-cult organization Association for the Defense of Families and Individuals (ADFI) launched an investigation and sent a former member to warn cultists living in Martinique.

Perhaps the most influential dissenter was Di Mambro's son, Eli. In 1990, when Eli was 29, he learned that many of the mystical feats his father performed during Solar Temple rituals were nothing more than holograms, laser lights, and sound effects being orchestrated behind the scenes. Eli was outspoken about his findings, as well as his belief that the masters in Zurich were just another instance of smoke and mirrors. Order of the Solar Temple leaders tried to justify these magic tricks as stunts to keep less-awakened temple members in the fold, but about 15 members defected along with Eli.

Meanwhile, Di Mambro's 12-year-old "cosmic" daughter Emmanuelle, who was supposedly conceived by the Gods in Israel, was acting out and distancing herself from her great responsibility of bringing in the New Age. Emmanuelle, who was intelligent and spoke five languages, had become more interested in pop culture than her father's secretive sect. She was also growing rebellious against her coddled and sheltered upbringing, and her father's mandate that she wear a helmet and gloves to protect her aura. Emmanuelle had another duty: Use her "powers" to open doors and windows on command. But this open-sesame trick was just another tactic for Di Mambro to convince his followers of his supernatural powers, as a button concealed beneath his cloak actually moved objects when Emmanuelle yelled *Ouvrez!* [Open!]

Then, in March 1993, the Order of the Solar Temple was thrust into the mainstream and had all of Canada talking, according to a Canadian Broadcasting Corporation reporter. Three members, including Luc Jouret, were arrested after trying to buy three guns with silencers. Police had tapped their phone lines and were investigating the group for making threatening anonymous calls to members of the Canadian National Assembly, taking part in a conspiracy to bomb First Nations reserves, and releasing explosions at Hydro-Quebec transmission towers (the same company that had hired Jouret to give employee pep talks).

For the gun charges, Jouret, along with insurance salesman Hermann Delorme and Hydro-Quebec project manager Jean-Pierre Vinet, were fined $750. Jouret left for Europe and was never seen in Canada again.

Many experts believe that a growing rift between Di Mambro and Jouret, pressure to disclose finances, and Eli Di Mambro's defection led the cult down a path toward mass suicide. Although the Order of the Solar Temple was always transparent about their apocalyptic beliefs, the idea of "transit" didn't start until the defections and other problems started in the early 1990s.

As previously mentioned, groups with fatalistic tendencies can turn violent when they are under threat and become all-consumed with thoughts of death.

Psychiatrist and cult researcher Robert Jay Lifton writes in a *World Policy Journal* article, "Since the death anxiety can only be eased by the disappearance of evil and the evil can only be overcome by a realization of the apocalypse, there develops a hungry impatience for its realization. The evil being confronted is viewed as something like an enemy army, which must not only be defeated but, since ever ready to regroup, annihilated." He adds, "Apocalyptic violence becomes the ultimate form of regeneration and becomes equated with immortality." Some of these groups, including the Order of the Solar Temple, as well as another group closely studied by Lifton, Aum Shinrikyo, decide that they must destroy the world in order to save it.

OCTOBER 4 TO 5, 1994

Turning now to our lead international report, police in Switzerland and Canada have a gruesome mystery on their hands tonight. In Switzerland, they're looking into what appears to be a mass murder-suicide. So far 48 people are known to be dead there; four are Canadians. Their bodies were found in a number of chalets in several Alpine villages. Yesterday, two bodies were found in burned-out townhouse in Quebec. Police there are convinced there is a connection.

—October 5, 1994, host Bob Oxley for CBC Radio's
The World at Six

In Cheiry, Switzerland, a farming town with just 275 residents, late-night revelers spotted the flames shooting out of the roof of a nearby farmhouse and alerted the volunteer fire department. Once the fire was extinguished, the firefighters found more than charred furniture and fallen support beams inside the building. In a bed was the body of a man with a plastic bag fastened over his head—the home's owner who had bought the property four years earlier. The police were called, as well as investigating judge Andre Piller, who made the 40-minute ride to the village from Fribourg.

Soon after entering the home, Piller and his fellow investigators noticed propane tanks, plastic bags filled with gasoline, and incendiary devices—even more proof that this fire was no accident.

Perhaps the man in bed, Albert Giacobino, had committed suicide by fire. But what about that bullet hole in his head concealed under that plastic bag, and no guns to be found?

Investigators searched the home for hours, venturing into a garage that had been converted into a chapel. There they found numerous briefcases containing ideological treatises that revealed the group's name as the Order of the Solar Temple. These documents had been sent to 60 scholars, reporters, and government officials as well. "To all those who can still understand the voice of wisdom," was the salutation of one of the letters. "May our love and peace accompany you during terrible tests of the apocalypse that await you. Know that from where we will be, we will always hold out arms open to receive those who are worthy of joining us."

Around 4 a.m., weary investigators located a trapdoor concealed in the wooden paneling that revealed a corridor lined with gasoline canisters. In a room at the end, investigators discovered a room decorated with red fabric. A painting of Jesus Christ with a rose above his head hung on the wall, and 18 bodies were laid before the son of God. Their corpses had been arranged in a star shape, and they wore red, black, white, and gold robes to indicate their rank in this secret order. Like Giacobino, they had plastic bags over their heads that, once removed, revealed burnt hair, melted skin, blistered lips, and bullet holes. They had been given drugs and tranquilizers; defensive wounds indicated that some fought back before being shot in the head. The room was silent except for a voice recorded on a cassette tape that was droning on about astrological concepts. Another door led to an octagonal room with mirrored walls and three more dead bodies. A final room was found containing a final corpse.

As Piller and his team uncovered room after room of bodies in Giacobino's chalet, a sleepless tourist about 60 miles away in Granges-sur-Salvan, Switzerland, spotted a fire from his hotel room window. Like the Cheiry fires, incendiary devices ignited gasoline to send three buildings up in flames. Unlike the Cheiry fires, the apparatuses worked properly. Of the 25 bodies later recovered, many were burned beyond recognition and had to be identified using dental records. Five of the dead were children, the youngest just four years old. In one of the downstairs bedrooms, police found a boy hugging a girl in a red dress, whom police said appeared to be "almost smiling" in her final resting place. Among the dead were Robert Ostiguy, mayor of a small Canadian town called Richelieu, and his wife Francoise, and Joce-Lyne Grand'Maison, senior reporter for *Le Journal de Quebec*.

Back in Canada, a fire in a Morin Heights lodge killed Order of the Solar Temple members Gerry and Colette Genoud. Two days later, the bodies of the Dutoit family were found stuffed in a storage closet of the burned-out building.

Tony and Nicky Dutoit wore red and gold medallions around their necks engraved with "TS" for Temple Solaire. Tony, who previously arranged lighting and other details for Di Mambro's rituals before falling out with the cult leader, had been beaten over the head with a blunt object, stabbed 50 times in the chest, and had his throat slit. Nicky, who sewed the group's ceremonial capes and other outfits, had been stabbed numerous times in the back, throat, and breast. And Emmanuel, the three-month-old baby whom the Dutoits had dared to give the same name as Di Mambro's "cosmic" daughter, had been stabbed in the chest, leading to 20 gashes in his heart. The baby had been bled white and then stuffed behind a water heater. Di Mambro, who had instructed the Dutoits not to have the child, believed baby Emmanuel was the polar opposite of his daughter descended from the Gods. He declared the baby the Antichrist, and ordered the entire Dutoit family killed in the days leading up to the 1994 chalet fires. Canadian police determined the Genouds had invited the Dutoits to dinner, and two associates sent to Canada by Di Mambro ambushed the family as they walked in the door. The accomplices then drove the Dutoits' car to the Montreal airport and returned to Switzerland, leaving the Genouds to clean up the blood and mess made by the triple-murder, before killing themselves three days later.

Four days after the fires, not all of the bodies had been identified. Arrest warrants were issued for Joseph Di Mambro and Luc Jouret, who were suspected to have run out with the cult's money. But both of their charred remains were identified and pulled from the burned chalet, ending a worldwide manhunt.

What were investigators to make of the motive? Letters recovered at Granges-sur-Salvan, written by Jouret and Di Mambro, declared that the group had "died in joy and plenitude"—and on their own terms. Law enforcement initially believed that the cult leaders might have killed their followers, especially when they discovered that one of Jouret's associates opened an Australian bank account with a $93 million deposit a year earlier, and found that the groups' real estate profiles included lavish beach and mountain getaways. But, when Di Mambro and Jouret were found among the dead as well, investigators believed that the leaders had orchestrated the killings and executions, and that their motive was to ascend to Sirius with their followers.

Order of the Solar Temple members didn't want to be left behind. A well-dressed, middle-aged woman went into a Swiss police station after the fires, upset that she hadn't been burned beyond recognition, too.

The Swiss government's investigation, completed a year and a half after the fires, concluded that only about 15 out of 53 people willingly committed suicide. The largest number of members were "assisted"—drugged and then shot in the head by another member who later took his or her own life—and at least 30 people were murdered as part of a death pact—a mass assassination—that was orchestrated by Di Mambro. Those who refused—the traitors—were shot repeatedly to death. One of the possible traitors was Eli Di Mambro, Di Mambro's whistleblowing son who revealed his father's spiritual trickery. Eli, who had been estranged from his father, was likely lured to his father's home and held against his will before dying in the fire. And families of the victims believe that the group did not die with their leaders but was still active and planning future "transits."

THE DEPARTURES CONTINUE

The families were right. On December 20, 1995, 14 months after the fires in Switzerland, abandoned cars were found in a remote region of the French Alps near Grenoble. A police helicopter flying over the forest spotted the 16 bodies, positioned in a star shape just like their predecessors had been. The dead included three children, and these Order of the Solar Temple cultists had been sedated, asphyxiated, and shot before being burned by a fire fueled by forest brush and surrounding trees. Letters left behind indicated the dead wanted to "see another world," and investigators concluded this was a collective murder that likely happened on the Winter Solstice a few days before the corpses were found. This second wave of Solar Temple deaths reignited media interest in this secret, esoteric group, and concerned law-enforcement officials. The millennium was fast approaching. How many more Order of the Solar Temple faithful were out there? How many of them would kill themselves in transit?

Didier Quèze, who lived with his family in St. Casimir, Canada, admitted he was a cult member in media interviews. But he also claimed that the cult had disbanded after the first wave of deaths in Switzerland.

In March 1997, Quèze, with his wife, Chantal Goupillot, spent days in agony in their home, switching on and off the propane tanks inside their home, and debating whether or not they should respect the wishes of their three teenagers, aged 13, 14, and 16, who did not want to die with their family. The teens would not be among the five bodies—of course, arranged in a star shape—pulled from the rubble of their two-story home on

March 23. Instead, they'd be found drugged and sleeping in a shed behind the house that was blanketed with inches of snow.

Even though Canadian prosecutors believe the teens had started the fire that killed their parents, another cult couple, and their grandmother (who had died after taking pills and being burned in the fire), prosecutors declined to file charges against them, citing the psychological effects of growing up in a cult and the influence of sedatives.

"Considering the exceptional circumstances and the age of the adolescents, there is good reason to wonder about responsibility, to the point where I believe that no jury or judge ... would hold them responsible," prosecutor Mario Tremblay said in court. "For this reason, I don't believe it appropriate to lay charges." The teens eventually moved to France to live with family, according to media reports.

The five dead in St. Casimir brought the number of Order of the Solar Temple deaths to 74. The body count remains at that number today (though police in the Canary Islands announced in 1998 that they had stopped a mass suicide planned by a Solar Temple chapter, which later turned out to be an unaffiliated cult led by a German motivational speaker named Heide Fittkau-Garthe).

EUROPE'S CULT PANIC LAUNCHES

Following the Order of the Solar Temple deaths, European society responded in a similar way that Americans did after photos and video reports flooded in from Jonestown in Guyana—in an all-out moral panic. The moral panic theory, developed in the 1970s, is a concept that society produces a fearful and overexaggerated response to societal problems (such as fearing poisoned Halloween candy or believing the fantasy board game *Dungeons and Dragons* is a gateway to satanism). Researchers James T. Richardson and Massimo Introvigne write that moral panics are "out of proportion to the actual threat" and are "often based on folk statistics that are passed from media to media and may ultimately inspire political measures." Cults, with differing beliefs and outsider status, are the quintessential target of moral panics. Newspaper and magazine articles, ranging from highbrow think pieces to lowbrow tabloid coverage, exploded in the years following the Solar Temple suicides (religions professor Susan J. Palmer noted that these headlines were still going strong into the summer of 2001 until the "Muslim problem" became a focus).

While the Swiss suggested the Order of the Solar Temple might be outlawed in their country, the French maintained after the Grenoble deaths that not much could be done to prevent cult activity in their country due to constitutional protection for religion.

"If it goes on like this, if the laws aren't there, it will be like the Wild West," Jean Vuarnet, the Olympian whose wife and son died, said during a television interview. "People will organize militias against these groups. Is that what lawmakers want?"

But with Joseph Di Mambro, Luc Jouret, and many core members of the Order of the Solar Temple dead and therefore unable to answer for their crimes, authorities had to pursue other avenues for justice. In 2001, renowned Franco-Swiss orchestra conductor and admitted cult member Michel Tabachnik was charged with participation in a criminal association related to the 16 deaths in France—the only major trial connected to the Solar Temple. With 50 witnesses ready to testify and many victims set to attend, the proceedings were moved to a former museum to accommodate the numbers.

Tabachnik, who denied being brainwashed, had attended two important meetings in 1994 when the cultists decided that the time was ripe for transit, according to prosecutors. The murders, suicides, and immolations took place 11 days after that second meeting. The government also argued that Tabachnik convinced other Solar Temple members of their elite status and celestial mission through his New Age and esoteric writings for the group. At trial, a singer named Evelyne Brunner-Bellaton, who was a follower of Di Mambro's from 1979 through 1985, testified that Tabachnik was Di Mambro's "crown prince" who could step in for him during ceremonies if need be, and that Tabachnik was poised to become Di Mambro's successor until the two had a falling out. (Brunner-Bellaton also told the court that she was convinced there was a leader above Di Mambro, and that she overheard another cultist discussing with Di Mambro that the cultists would be committing suicide en masse, voluntarily or otherwise).

Tabachnik protested that he was a victim of Di Mambro's manipulation, not a co-conspirator, and was later cleared of the charge that could have sent him to prison for 10 years. The verdict was appealed by French prosecutors, and five years later an appellate court upheld the decision. (Swiss authorities investigating the 1994 deaths in the Swiss Alps could not find a link between Tabachnik and the fires). After his acquittal, Tabachnik continued to work as conductor for orchestras around the world.

If French courts couldn't convict those associated with the Order of the Solar Temple, they were able to make the country a much less appealing home for cult leaders. In June 2000, the French National Assembly passed a bill that banned cults outright. Minister of Justice Elisabeth Guigou praised the bill as "a significant advance giving a democratic state the legal tools efficiently to fight groups abusing its core values." But France's move was viewed as unpopular and draconian to the international human rights community, and the bill never came to fruition.

The following year, however, France adopted a law that introduced the idea of brainwashing into French common law, creating a new class of misdemeanor called *abus de faiblesse* ("abuse of weakness"). Abus de faiblesse could be used to prosecute a cult leader for the various ways they might abuse their followers, such as physical and sexual abuse, fraud, denial of food or medical treatment, promotion of suicide, and mind control, punishable by up to five years in prison and 750,000 euro in damages.

Even before this new legislation was passed, France had an anti-cult ministry known as *Mission interministérielle de lutte contre les sectes* ("Interministerial Mission in the Fight Against Cults"), or MILS, and a "bad cut" list of 200 groups, which included religious organizations recognized in other countries, such as the Jehovah's Witnesses and Pentecostal Christian denominations.

MILS was disbanded in 2002 and replaced with a new government agency, called *Mission interministérielle de vigilance et de lutte contre les dérives sectaires* ("Interministerial mission of vigilance and fight against sectarian excesses"), or MIVILUDES. While MILS fought against cults, MIVILUDES pledged to weed out "sectarian deviances" that threatened traditional French values. The government-funded cult help group ADFI, which has 50 locations throughout the country, freely admits to sending spies to cult meetings. Susan J. Palmer, who has found in her research that the French exempt Jewish and Muslim sects, and that cultists are often ostracized, summed it up in short: "Several effective strategies have been put in place to rid France of its annoyingly irrational spiritual and philosophical minorities."

More than 20 years after the last Solar Temple death, MIVILUDES lives on, offering general information and local resources on French cults, producing annual reports on cult activity, and issuing periodic alerts. In June 2011, MIVILUDES chairman George Fenech paid a concerned visit to the southwestern French village of Bugarach, a hippie enclave in the mountains where spiritual seekers had been arriving to prepare for the end of the Mayan calendar on December 21, 2012. The village was expected to swell to thousands of apocalypse anticipators. Bugarach, home to 200 permanent residents and the iconic Pic de Bugarach, the "upside-down mountain," has been attracting the spiritually curious since the 1960s, some of whom believe the single mountain peak houses a spaceship. According to *Times*, though Fenech dismissed the apocalyptic prediction as a "hodgepodge of bad astrophysics," he traveled to Bugarach to meet with police and warn about "the horror of the dramas which cults have caused in recent years with their doctrines that provoke extreme anxiety."

Bugarach topped a tongue-and-cheek Texas newspaper's list of the five best places to watch the world end, beating out a Turkish village named Sirince, where the Virgin Mary ascended to heaven, and Megiddo, a village in northern Israel that had already seen a biblical Armageddon. The influx of end-time visitors led to a rise in local property prices, as well as an uptick in what *Huntsville Item* (Texas) articles described as "half-naked ramblers climbing up the mountain ringing bells" that led to local authorities blocking access to Pic de Bugarach until doomsday had passed.

The most recent MIVILUDES annual report found a slight increase in the number of cult tips in 2016: 2,323. "The craze for alternative therapies, for personal development methods, for pseudo-psychotherapies, for alternative pedagogies offers new opportunities for movements and leaders seeking to exercise a hold on their followers," the report reads in French, adding that top cult recruit subjects include Europe's refugee crisis and environmental concerns.

AUM SHINRIKYO

If you inhale the mysterious vapor,

You will fall with bloody vomit from your mouth,

Sarin, sarin, sarin,

The chemical weapon.

> —From "Song of Sarin the Magician," printed in
> a 1994 Aum Shinrikyo pamphlet

Umbrellas. Newspapers. Not an unusual sight on a packed subway train during rush hour. Who knows how many people riding the trains in New York, Paris, Hong Kong, or Moscow at this very moment are carrying the very same items.

But these familiar sights had a far more sinister purpose on the morning of March 20, 1995, in Japan. During the Monday morning rush hour, five men boarded trains at different locations on the vast Tokyo Underground. They carried packages of sarin, a deadly synthetic nerve agent first developed by Nazi scientists that has the potential to be hundreds of times deadlier than cyanide.

With the trains heading toward Kasumigaseki, the centralized government district, the men placed the bags on the floor of the subway car and punctured them with the tips of their umbrellas. They hopped off the train at the next stop, calmly making their way to an escape car. A syringe was in their pockets with an antidote to reverse the deadly nerve agent, just in case they had poisoned themselves. The attackers left little more in their wake than the sarin packages, which were wrapped in communist and religious newspapers to throw off the police. Over the next few minutes, the sarin gas dissipated through the air and spread through the cars.

It was a silent scene of devastation that morning. Sarin constricts the airway, so the victims couldn't even scream out in pain as they gasped for breath and thrashed around on the ground, blood streaming out of their noses and mouths. At first, the trains kept running, spreading the chemical weapon throughout the system. Two subway workers, including a deputy station master, died after removing one of the sarin packages from a train. Above ground, emergency responders treated thousands of stunned victims who had no idea what had happened to them and how they had gotten so sick so quickly.

The attacks would eventually kill 13 people and injure and traumatize thousands more. Sarin also prevents oxygen from reaching the brain, and some people who survived ended up in vegetative comas or confined to wheelchairs. One woman had to have both of her eyes surgically removed after her contact lenses permanently fused to her eyeballs.

Survivor Atsushi Sakahara, who was riding one of the subway cars that the sarin was released in, would later tell the Associated Press that he first noticed that his eyes were going in and out of focus. Seeing the newspaper-wrapped package on the floor, he instinctively sensed something was amiss, and moved to the next car. Looking back, he saw a man had lost consciousness. Sakahara, then in his late twenties, fled the subway and took a taxi to work, where his vision gradually got darker and darker, as if he didn't need sunglasses to look directly at the sun.

The attack devastated the massive Tokyo metropolitan area, home to 32 million, and sent shockwaves of fear through the famously safe country. Japan was still reeling from the devastating 7.2-magnitude earthquake in Kobe two months earlier, which killed nearly 5,000 people and leveled buildings and highways. Slow disaster relief left victims without food, water, and shelter for days.

Who was responsible for unleashing this chemical weapon, which had only been used before in a large-scale attack by Iraqi President Saddam Hussein against the Kurds? Turns out, it wasn't a terrorist organization from a far-flung corner of the world that was responsible for turning Tokyo into a scene out of a horror film, but highly educated scientists and doctors from within the country. They had orders from their half-blind guru, Shoko Asahara, that they took very seriously: Launch their country, and the world, into an apocalypse.

The cult, called Aum Shinrikyo, or "supreme truth," started as a yoga school out of Asahara's Tokyo apartment in the mid-1980s. In the decade that followed, Asahara gathered thousands of followers for his movement, which combined elements of Buddhism, Hinduism, Christianity, and New Age religions. And while many cult leaders predict the end of the world, Asahara perhaps went the furthest to set the end-times in motion, building a compound at the foot of Mount Fuji, the country's highest peak some 60 miles southwest of Tokyo where his brightest recruits could manufacture their own biological and chemical weapons.

Shoko Asahara wasn't waiting around for the apocalypse, he was making it happen. And, he promised, only his followers would make it out alive.

BECOMING SHOKO ASAHARA

Chizuo Matsumoto, who would later assume the name Shoko Asahara, was born in a remote and rural area of southern Japan in 1955. He was the sixth of seven children, and his poor family made what little money they had weaving *tatami* mats, a traditional Japanese floor covering made from rice straw.

Congenital glaucoma left Asahara with only partial vision from a young age. His family sent him to live at a school for the blind, along with two other siblings. Asahara stayed there until he was 20 years old.

Robert Jay Lifton, a psychiatrist who interviewed many former members of Aum Shinrikyo for his book *Destroying the World in Order to Save It: Aum Shinrikyo, Apocalyptic Violence, and the New Global Terrorism*, wrote that "no adult is a mere product of childhood. There is always a forward momentum to the self that does not follow simple cause and effect." Asahara, who would mumble incoherently during his lengthy trial following the Tokyo attack, has been described as bright and charismatic, but also had delusional and paranoid tendencies that would change the course of his life in later years. He achieved good grades, had a passion for drama, and excelled at judo, the Japanese martial art that has the end goal of taking down your opponent.

Asahara was also manipulative and cunning. He would use his partial sight to his advantage, offering to run errands for his fully blind classmates for the right price. He had aspirations of becoming the Japanese prime minister and tried to jump-start his political career by running for class head at school. He was never elected, despite multiple campaigns and his efforts to bribe his colleagues with sweets in exchange for their votes. And although Asahara has been remembered as a manipulative bully, his teachers also recalled his ability to be kind, especially to his younger brother.

According to intelligence expert John Parachini, aggression was a way for Asahara to be assertive and "counter his sense of inferiority." After finishing school, Asahara moved to Tokyo, where he said he planned to study for college entrance exams. He hoped to be accepted to a law or medical school but was never admitted. Whether he actually took the tests, however, is unknown. Instead, Asahara studied Chinese medicine and opened a clinic with the financial help of his new wife's family. But in 1982, Asahara was caught and convicted of selling fake herbs. The fines bankrupted him, and this professional failure led to his increased interest and study of religion and mysticism.

New religious movements were cropping up across Japan in the 1980s, a phenomenon attributed to a decline in spirituality leading up to World War II, the economic downturn, and a more general dip in moral values. When Asahara was 26, he joined a new religious movement called Agon-shu, which was led by the guru Seiyu Kiriyama. This was Asahara's introduction to Buddhist teachings, and he spent the next few years gleaning lessons that he would later use in his own movement. But unlike Kiriyama, who died in 2016 and devoted his life to advancing peace and education around the world, Asahara ultimately wouldn't use the Buddhist teachings for good.

This seems like a good place to pause and explain a bit more about traditional Buddhism, which is quite different from Asahara's interpretations. Buddhism is an Eastern religion that started around 2,600 years ago by Siddhartha Gautama, a former prince who renounced the world and would eventually become the Buddha after reaching enlightenment. Throughout the centuries, different Buddhist schools developed, including Theravada and Mahayana. Many, though not all, Buddhist schools place an emphasis on meditation as a path to enlightenment. Buddhists don't pray to a personal God, but instead work toward ending suffering by following the Buddha's teachings. At the core of the Buddha's teachings are the four noble truths, which pinpoint the cause of suffering and offer a prescription to end it (reaching nirvana) by following the eightfold path, a code of conduct that includes right speech and right mindfulness. There were an estimated 488 million Buddhists worldwide in

2010, according to the Pew Research Center, which expects the religion to grow to 511 million by 2030. Though Japan is one of 10 countries around the world with the highest percentage of Buddhists, the religion has been on the decline since the end of World War II. And though there are always exceptions, Buddhism is generally considered a peaceful religion that stresses compassion and nonviolence.

In 1984, Asahara founded Aum Shinsen no Kai. *Aum* is a sacred word and sound in Eastern religions that is often chanted, while *Shinsen no Kai* means something along the lines of a "circle of divine hermits" or "wizards." In the early years, Aum was a yoga and meditation school that Asahara operated out of his apartment. Asahara was a skilled yoga practitioner, and his fledgling group had its first brush with fame the following year when a photo of Asahara appearing to levitate high off the ground with his legs in full lotus position was printed in a Japanese occult magazine called *Twilight Zone*.

"My anti-gravity experiments have kept me aloft for no more than three seconds so far. But the period is increasing steadily. Within a year, my body should be able to fly at will," Asahara told the magazine.

Though it is generally agreed that the photo of Asahara hovering was staged, the promise of flight isn't that uncommon in some religious offshoots. Maharishi Mahesh Yogi, who founded Transcendental Meditation, claimed to be able to fly, and charged his followers thousands of dollars for access to his Yogic Flying courses. (The Maharishi, dubbed the Giggling Guru and a source of inspiration for the Beatles and numerous other celebrities, died in 2008. Transcendental Meditation, or TM, claims to have taught mantra meditation to millions. Critics have dismissed this enterprise as a cult business; at the time of the guru's death, the group had $300 million in assets in the US alone.)

Asahara instructed his followers to increase energy and circulation in the body through meditation and breathing exercises, and advised them to rid themselves of worldly interests and desires. In later years, Japanese television would show Aum followers trying to lift off the ground by bouncing up and down on their backside.

Asahara rounded out the mid-eighties by wandering Japan as a homeless monk and studying Buddhism and Hinduism in the Himalayas. Along the way, Asahara believed that Shiva— one of the major deities of Hinduism who is associated with the destruction of evil—appeared and instructed him to lead a battle of good against evil. In 1986, after spending four or five days in meditation, Asahara claimed that he reached "final enlightenment." Although he never explained what "final enlightenment" actually meant, it's generally agreed upon that enlightenment—which Buddhists often describe as "waking up" to the human condition—can take a lifetime, if not multiple lifetimes, to achieve. (And it's generally not a thing you brag about having accomplished to others.)

In an interview with *Tricycle: The Buddhist Review*, Lifton explains it didn't really matter if Asahara achieved this heightened state of being or not—"because he didn't belong to any reputable religious institution, he wasn't responsible to anybody or anything."

"But the act was convincing to his followers. And, in some way, it was convincing to himself. There's a strange psychology with some people that enables them to believe in their own version of events and simultaneously maintain a whole manipulative, con-man side. The combination can be persuasive," Lifton said.

Whether finally enlightened or not, Asahara spent his time in India meeting with established Buddhist teachers from recognized schools whose teachings have been passed down for millennia, including the 14th His Holiness the Dalai Lama, the Tibetan Buddhist leader, as well as the influential teacher Kalu Rinpoche. He also met religious dignitaries in Sri Lanka, a predominantly Buddhist country. Asahara made a point of collecting as many photographs with as many of these influential people as possible for future Aum Shinrikyo marketing materials. Asahara would later claim that the Dalai Lama told him "What I've done for Buddhism in Tibet, you will do for Buddhism in Japan." After the Tokyo attack, His Holiness acknowledged meeting with Asahara but denied giving him such a lofty mission.

Despite his delusions of spiritual grandeur, those who met Asahara during the 1980s recalled him as smart, funny, and sane, while at the same time unsophisticated and unrestrained. It would be these charismatic attributes and ability to be what Lifton describes as an "extraordinarily dignified and composed teacher," not his apocalyptic teachings, that would help his organization grow to include thousands of followers around the world.

AUM SUPREME TRUTH

Back from the Himalayas, Asahara renamed his group Aum Shinrikyo, or "supreme truth." Aum Shinrikyo's philosophy was based on a combination of Asahara's interpretation of Tibetan Buddhism, Hinduism, and Christianity, as well as some of the disastrous prophecies that the French physician and seer Nostradamus predicted in the sixteenth century. As Asahara developed his guru persona, he started claiming that he was the first enlightened person since the Buddha. Every guru needs a look: Asahara's was a long beard, flowing hair, and colorful robes. And a guru needs his followers: Asahara found his through university appearances and his books.

Asahara's new flock were the young and disenchanted, and Aum started recruiting new members from elite universities and upper-class families who were looking for purpose in life that they hadn't found in the workplace or through material possessions, and who likely lacked a religious upbringing. With Aum, they didn't have to question the purpose of life or make their own decisions—that's what Asahara was there for, to give them what one follower called a "true blueprint" toward raising their spiritual IQ.

And, as Asahara became increasingly preoccupied with putting the apocalypse in motion, his cult specifically targeted university chemistry, physics, and engineering departments for the best and brightest minds they could coerce.

Aum also used popular culture to reach new members, including science fiction magazines (remember the levitating photo?), Japanese comics called *manga*, and video games.

In "From Mysticism to Murder," Robert Lifton recounts some of the experiences that Aum followers told him:

> *People had frequent visionary experiences, many of which had to do with seeing bright lights—that seemed to be their mystical logo. From very early on, the word among people who had undergone training with Asahara was that it was extraordinarily intense, extraordinarily rewarding .... They describe experiencing high energy. And that energy itself took on a kind of mystical feeling because it really meant life power, immortality power ...*

Asahara borrowed practices from Tibetan Buddhist traditions, including prostrations, or moving from a standing position to prone position on the ground, an act performed in succession by Buddhists to purify negative karma. Another significant influence was the concept of *phowa*, the idea that a person's consciousness is released through the top of their head after death, as well as devotion to a guru to progress to buddhahood.

Asahara's notion of karma—the law of cause and effect that affects different aspects of our lives—was also fundamentally flawed and quite different from the mainstream Buddhist and Hindu definitions that teach that one's karma can be changed through our actions and spiritual practice. For Asahara, everyone in the world who had not joined his movement had irreversibly permanent bad karma. Exterminating the world of these hopeless souls was a compassionate act in Asahara's mind, because their deaths would give them a pure and clean slate in their next life. This idea wasn't shared by all of Aum's members, but Asahara was the guru, so the teachings were thrust upon his followers as he became more paranoid and obsessed with the impending Armageddon, which he predicted happening in 1996 or between 1999 and 2003. Asahara also taught that Aum members had the unique ability to separate their body and consciousness, an important attribute that would come in handy during the end times, when they would be able to withstand a higher amount of heat than regular, unenlightened humans.

Aum Shinrikyo displayed many of the classic signs of brainwashing. Cult members were deprived of enough food and sleep, forced to listen to tapes of Asahara singing on repeat, and given psychedelics such as LSD. Asahara also claimed that members could speed up their path to enlightenment. These shortcuts came at a price: $250 for the opportunity to drink Asahara's bath water, thousands more for a concoction laced with Asahara's blood, and a whopping $10,000 for access to an electrode helmet that claimed to pick up the guru's brainwaves. Many Aum members lived communally and wore different colors of clothing to correspond with their spiritual progress.

Aum also promised medical cures for diseases and conditions, luring in patients who felt that conventional medicine had failed them. In one case, a woman with Parkinson's was treated at an Aum institute for six months using a combination of "medicine" prescribed by cult physicians and "thermotherapy" treatments in the form of scalding hot water. She was later told that she wouldn't be cured unless she gave 45 million yen—nearly half a million dollars—to the cult.

Japanese journalist Shoko Egawa, who covered Aum Shinrikyo, would later tell *Wired* that the cult members "lived in a purely imaginary world ... one that combined primeval fear with a computer-controlled, cartoon version of reality.

The first death attributed to Aum Shinrikyo happened in 1988 when a cultist died, supposedly suffering a heart attack after a long and intense meditation session. At the time, Aum was in the process of applying for legal recognition as a religion, which would open up opportunities for tax breaks and little government oversight. Fearing that the cultist's death might jeopardize this status, the cult secretly disposed of the body. The following year, a member planning to leave Aum who had also witnessed that first death was killed. Aum defectors would later report that any perceived disobedience was severely punished, if not by death, through solitary confinement or torture tactics such as electric shocks and being hung upside down.

In 1989, Aum ended up receiving legal status as a religion, but not without a bit of wrangling. When it looked like things might not be going the cult's way, Aum members campaigned and protested until the authorities gave in.

Aum Shinrikyo saw increased scrutiny in the 1980s after rumors swirled of missing members and abuse. Following these early deaths and unfavorable media attention, concerned relatives organized a victim's advocacy group and retained civil rights attorney Tsutsumi Sakamoto to investigate the cult and represent families hoping to rescue their children. In November 1989, Sakamoto disappeared suddenly, along with his wife and 14-month-old son. Although Aum was suspected to be involved, the cult wasn't officially investigated at the time, partially because authorities may have been concerned about the groups' rights as a religion, the *New York Times* reported. Following the Tokyo subway attack, a former Aum member was arrested and charged with the Sakamoto family murders. Information from former cult members led to a massive search, which eventually turned up the remains of Sakamoto, his wife, and baby in three separate rural areas of Japan. Nearly 1,000 law-enforcement officers had combed the main Japanese island, with Japanese television stations reporting their progress live throughout the day. Due to new information offered up by cultists, police believed that cult assassins had broken into the Sakamotos' apartment, injecting their victims with a drug before hitting them with a hammer and strangling them.

THE SUPREME STATE

One more major event would occur before Aum Shinrikyo became even more insular and separate from Japanese society. In 1990, Asahara—who still had aspirations, even premonitions, of becoming a Japanese political leader—ran for Parliament along with a few other cult members. Their performance at the polls was dismal. After growing up blind and failing to gain entrance to university, this was the last straw for Asahara. If he couldn't make it in mainstream Japanese society, he'd have to get to work and create his own separate state.

Following Asahara's embarrassing defeat at the polls, Aum retreated into its own world, and Asahara's rhetoric ratcheted up as well.

The guru started teaching that the world was on the brink of World War III. The United States would decimate the Buddhist world, leveling Japan using nuclear, chemical, and biological weapons. Only those associated with Aum Shinrikyo would have pure enough karma to survive, and Asahara taught that cult members should lovingly welcome the end of the world.

Asahara had an axe to grind with Japan as well, and taught that Japan would suffer for persecuting him, just as the Jews suffered for persecuting Jesus Christ.

According to Asahara, Aum was being targeted precisely because they were the only group capable of saving the world from chaos.

As Asahara became more paranoid and delusional, he became fixated on weapons, in particular the fantasy of developing and building a giant laser.

The cult got to work to prepare for World War III, and they had the funds to do it—Aum Shinrikyo's wealth had grown considerably over the last few years. They continued selling the meditation books and classes that were their initial bread and butter, but also diversified their business holdings, operating restaurants, electronic businesses, and having members sign over their estates. This initial cash flush paved the way for more lucrative business dealings, including land acquisitions that would allow Asahara to start building labs and buying equipment to start manufacturing weapons at Aum Shinrikyo's massive compound located at the foot of Mount Fuji. To avoid detection, these businesses were set up as separate corporations not directly linked to Aum.

With Aum Shinrikyo activity centered around the Mount Fuji compound, Asahara set up a shadow government that mirrored the Japanese state. High-ranking Aum leaders were named ministers of various wings, such as health and welfare, construction, and intelligence. Aum's health and welfare minister, Seiichi Endo, was studying graduate-level biology at Kyoto University when he joined Aum. Just weeks after Asahara's political dreams were dashed in 1990, Endo was at work in a lab growing a botulism microbe collected from a northern Japanese island.

With Aum, the young university graduates and dropouts who specialized in science, technology, and engineering now found themselves as big fish in a small pond, rather than vice versa in the real world. But this freedom to experiment and research without too many rules may have ultimately backfired. Due to the small number of cult members who had direct knowledge that Asahara wanted to develop biological, then chemical, weapons, this limited group had to rely on their own knowledge, research, and capabilities, which likely hindered their success in developing more potent strains of sarin and botulinum.

In the years leading up to the Tokyo attack, Aum experimented with biological weapons, including anthrax and Q fever, which were cheaper to manufacture than chemical agents such as sarin and had the potential to kill millions of people.

Aum Shinrikyo's massive cash flow also allowed the cult to acquire military equipment, including a Russian helicopter and missiles. Several buildings at the compound were dedicated to manufacturing germs, and Aum's labs would later be described in a *New York Times* article by William J. Broad as a "maze of lab gear, glassware, and guru photos."

At its peak, Aum Shinrikyo's membership was around 40,000, and the cult had friends in high places, including the government, judiciary, military, and press (though only 3,000 members lived communally). Aum's intelligence wing was also adept at brazen break-ins that gave them access to top-secret military information. On more than one occasion, Aum members broke into Mitsubishi Heavy Industries, an engineering and defense company that designed, among other things, nuclear power plants. Aum was able to pull off the heist because they were given employee uniforms and access by cult members who worked there. Once inside the Hiroshima plant, the cultists downloaded encrypted files with information that they could use for their own weapon development.

1990 TO 1995 ATTACKS

Though Aum would successfully produce a strain of sarin that managed to kill people, there was a naive and bumbling element to the cult's capabilities and production, despite all their wealth and planning. Aum's scientists likely exposed themselves to the deadly agents they were working to make. The cult used an apprentice-style program to increase the number of people working on weapons development. This meant that cultists who previously worked in publishing and illustration now found themselves brandishing welders, which led to a number of injuries. In 1993, Aum members released anthrax spores into a building that did little more than stink up the air and kill a few plants and animals. Plans to purchase a giant laser from a company in California fell through because Aum wanted the custom-made, half-million-dollar laser to be available to them immediately. Aum was able to smuggle an AK-47 into the country, but only managed to make one copy of the assault rifle.

With biological weapons not working the way Asahara and his team had hoped, the guru turned to sarin, a highly toxic synthetic chemical that can be spread rapidly both through the air and by physical contact. According to Lifton, they thought of sarin as the "poor man's atomic bomb," and Aum Shinrikyo likely learned how to make it from a Russian expert who visited the cult's headquarters. (Aum had more than a significant presence in Russia, with some numbers putting Russian members at 30,000, far more than an estimated 10,000 Japanese followers.)

According to the Centers for Disease Control and Prevention, sarin and all nerve agents cause their toxic effects by preventing the proper operation of an enzyme that acts as the body's "off switch" for glands and muscles. Without this switch, the glands and muscles are constantly stimulated. People who are exposed to sarin may become fatigued. Other serious side effects include a change in heart rate and blood pressure, blurred vision, confusion, convulsions, and respiratory failure. Sarin doesn't have a color or taste, and quickly evaporates into vapor after exposing people to its deadly effects.

The cult tested the toxic chemicals at a 500,000-acre ranch that they had purchased in a desolate area hundreds of miles north of Perth, Australia, on land believed to contain uranium, a metal that can be enhanced to make nuclear weapons. But Asahara and 25 of his followers didn't travel lightly—or inconspicuously—down under. They were fined by

Australian authorities for attempting to ship toxic chemicals in containers marked "hand soap."

"Despite its nefarious activities, Aum did not seem to adopt even modest operational security procedures during this trip," Parachini writes. "Either its members believed that the rightness of their mission would safeguard them from the authorities or they were incredibly naïve."

Following this trip, most of the group was denied visas for a repeat visit to Australia. However, a few who eventually obtained visas returned to the ranch to test toxic agents on sheep.

Traces of sarin were found in 24 sheep carcasses at the ranch, which the cult had named Banjawarn. Locals from the desert town also witnessed a strange blast that sent a bright light through the air, causing the ground to shake enough to register 3.6 on the Richter scale—the level of a small earthquake.

The fact that Aum's biological and chemical weapons were never as potent as Asahara would have liked didn't stop the cult from carrying out an estimated 14 attacks between 1990 and 1995. Sprayers mounted on trucks released botulinum toxin near a US military base and Japanese government buildings. Their most deadly attack before the one in the Tokyo underground happened in the city of Matsumoto in 1994. Eight people were killed and hundreds more injured when Aum Shinrikyo sprayed sarin near an apartment complex where judges, who were set to rule on a land dispute they were involved in, resided. Local police investigated a local businessman, Yoshiyuki Kono, and his trial by media depicted him as the main suspect until after Aum's motives were revealed following the Tokyo attack.

In early 1995, Aum Shinrikyo attackers posing as joggers sprayed Hiroyuki Nagaoka with VX nerve gas as he was walking through his Tokyo neighborhood. Nagaoka was saved by his sweater and collar, which blocked most of the liquid from his skin. At the time, he didn't know that he had been attacked, but back at home, he lost his ability to see and felt as though his chest and lungs were on fire. He lost consciousness and thrashed around on the floor before being taken to the hospital, where a doctor recognized the signs of exposure to nerve gas. Nagaoka was targeted because he led a support group for parents whose children had joined Aum Shinrikyo. Nagaoka, who still experiences numbness on the right side of his body more than 20 years after the attack, didn't know for sure that the cultists were behind the attack until it was revealed at trial many years later.

On March 15, 1995, Aum Shinrikyo members carrying briefcases with the necessary alterations descended into the Tokyo subway station, intending to spray botulinum. Nothing happened; it's unclear if the biological weapon was intentionally left out or not.

Five days later, five attackers would board the subway trains in Tokyo with those newspaper-wrapped packages of sarin and their umbrellas, carrying out the deadly subway mission. If Shoko Asahara could have had his way, the attack would have been much deadlier. Working a tip that a police raid was planned for the cult's headquarters, Asahara hastily moved up the attack date, which was scheduled for November. If all had gone according to plan, Asahara would have released 70 tons of sarin over Tokyo from helicopters. Thousands, if not millions, could have been killed.

ARRESTS AND JAPAN'S TRIAL OF THE CENTURY

High-ranking Aum Shinrikyo members would be arrested in the months following the subway attack. Some members, including medical chief Ikuo Hayashi, confessed to their roles.

In May 1995, some 2,000 officers descended on the Aum Shinrikyo compound with warrants for 40 members, including Asahara. It took police four hours to track down the cult leader, who was found meditating in a secret room between the second and third floors of a building, dressed in purple robes. Responding law enforcement had expected the cult to retaliate and were appropriately outfitted in gas masks and protective suits on loan from the Japanese Self-Defense Forces. No additional sarin was found in Aum's labs, which were sealed off by police in the days following the subway attack. The raid did, however, turn up a written order in which Asahara decreed that the cult should start experimenting with sarin, as well as detailing missile fragments and new laboratories in the works.

With Asahara in jail, Fumihiro Joyu, a high-ranking Aum Shinrikyo member serving in Moscow, became the group's spokesperson. Despite the devastation Aum inflicted on Japan—and hoped to on the world—the group continues to operate under increased police surveillance and a law that requires them to contribute to victim compensation. (The group has maintained that these measures violate their civil rights as a religious organization.)

After the attack, Aum rebranded under the new name Aleph, and the group, with Joyu at the helm, started recruiting new members in 1997 and got back to work opening businesses and acquiring properties. Joyu tried to distance the group from Asahara and his violent acts, which eventually led to a split in 2003 after Joyu had Asahara's books and videos removed from Aleph's buildings. Asahara loyalists stayed with Aleph, and those who wanted to be done with their former guru followed Joyu, who started a new group called Hikari no Wa. Joyu maintains Hikari no Wa is a philosophy, not a religion. The group was surveilled along with Aleph until September 2017, when a Japanese court ruled in favor of Hikari and suspended surveillance against the cult, which has about 150 members.

The trials for Shoko Asahara, his ministers, and other high-ranking Aum members would become Japan's trial of the century, dragging on until 2018, when Japan's Supreme Court upheld a final appeal. Shoko Asahara was sentenced to death in 2004 following an eight-year trial. Asahara's state-appointed lawyers tried to distance Asahara from his followers, whom they say acted independently and not on their leader's orders. Asahara, who some say purposely acted crazy during his trial and accused the judge of zapping his brain with radiation, didn't answer questions coherently. When he was sentenced on numerous charges to death by hanging, the guru had to be forced on his feet by court guards. It took four hours for the judge to read the verdicts, and during this time Ashara smiled, yawned, snorted, mumbled to himself, and smelled his fingers.

All in all, 12 additional members of Aum Shinrikyo were sentenced to death for their crimes, and five more received life sentences. Lawyers representing Seiichi Endo, who helped manufacture sarin and was convicted of murder for the Tokyo and Matsumoto attacks, claimed that his mind was being controlled by Asahara, and that he had no idea what the deadly liquid would be used for. The trials dragged on for so long because three cultists were on the lam until 2011.

In March 2018, seven of the 13 Aum members on death row were transported from the Tokyo Detention Center to different prisons in preparation for their executions. Aleph and other groups, including Amnesty International, Japan Society for Cult Prevention and Recovery, and a coalition of Buddhists, asked that the men be spared. But on July 6, Japan ordered the executions of Asahara and six of his followers. The remaining death row cultists were put to death on July 26. Justice Minister Yoko Kamikawa, who ordered the executions, will be guarded for the rest of her life along with her immediate family, to protect them from retaliation.

Aum Shinrikyo's ability to acquire and manufacture weapons of mass destruction had serious international implications in a pre-9/11 world, with the sarin attacks serving as a wake-up call that do-it-yourself weapons were possible and that pathogens and other potentially deadly compounds weren't being safely regulated (all it took for Aum to get their hands on anthrax was a member's medical license). Fighting "germ terrorism" became a priority, and President Bill Clinton announced that the US would keep a stockpile of vaccines and antibiotics.

VX, the nerve agent that Aum members sprayed on their adversaries' necks while posing as joggers, was back in the limelight in late 2017, when the substance was used to assassinate Kim Jong-nam. Closed-circuit video surveillance captured the attack on North Korean leader Kim Jong-un's half-brother, who was approached by two women in a Malaysian airport who smeared a substance in his face. He died about 20 minutes later on his way to the hospital.

A few months later, a research paper warning of the use of VX in future attacks came from the unlikeliest coauthor: Tomomasa Nakagawa, one of the seven Aum Shinrikyo members executed for his role in the sarin attacks.

Incoherent or otherwise, many believe Asahara continued to guide Aleph until the time of his death. The cult, which has an estimated 1,500 members, seems to be up to their old tricks, attracting new, young members through yoga classes, failing to mention their violent history, and bilking followers out of thousands of dollars in membership fees. Other countries are far less tolerant of the cult. In 2016, Russia, which had a sizeable Aum membership, officially banned Aleph after the country's Supreme Court designated it a terrorist organization. Earlier that year, Montenegro deported nearly 60 foreign Aleph members whom officials said were staying in the country illegally.

CHAPTER 8

ROD FERRELL'S VAMPIRE CLAN

Roderrick (Rod) Farrell was a pale, skinny, stringy-haired high school dropout from a troubled family who sliced his arms, carved a demonic symbol on his chest, and found community through his assumed identity as a 500-year-old vampire. Heather Wendorf roamed the hallways of her Florida high school in long black clothes, a Barbie doll hanging from a noose off of her backpack. She insisted to her boyfriends that the best sex you could have happened after drinking blood.

The two met in 1995 when they were both living in Eustis, Florida, a small city of about 15,000 known as "America's Hometown," 30 miles north of Orlando. They shared an interest in the undead and dated for a spell. In December 1995, after Ferrell's mother discovered Rod and three other teens covered in blood in his bedroom, she moved him back to her hometown of Murray, Kentucky—one of many moves they made between the two states during Rod's young life. But Ferrell and Wendorf continued to keep in touch (and Heather's $80-a-month long-distance phone bills became a point of contention between her and her parents). Over seven months in 1996, Wendorf apparently told Ferrell that her parents were "hurting her." Ferrell decided to travel to Florida to rescue Wendorf, and then head to Louisiana. Along for the ride in the red Buick Skylark were his fellow vampire friends and members of his supposed cult, the Vampire Clan. They were Howard Scott Anderson, 16, Dana Cooper, 19, and Charity Keesee, 16, who wanted a clean start far away from Murray.

By Thanksgiving, Wendorf and Ferrell's lives would be irrevocably intertwined, and not just because of the "crossing over" vampire ceremony that Rod, then 16, performed on Heather, 15, in Eustis's Greenwood Cemetery. By the time the Vampire Clan left town, Heather's parents, Richard and Ruth Wendorf, had been bludgeoned to death with a crowbar, with a combined 50 wounds on their bodies. And, unlike their vampire assassins, they had no hope of coming back to life under the cover of darkness.

VINTAGE VAMPIRES

Unlike some of the more modern cults that claim to receive messages from God through alien encounters, the claim of vampires roaming America (as well as the rest of the world) has a much longer history. Many ancient civilizations feared some sort of blood-sucking demon, and our modern notion of the vampire can be traced back to tenth-century Slavic regions of Europe. New World settlers eventually brought this superstition with them across the Atlantic.

By the nineteenth century, tuberculosis, then known as "consumption" and sometimes referred to as the "White Plague," had killed one in seven people who had ever lived. In an era before the discovery that the *Mycobacterium tuberculosis* bacteria was easily spread through the air, some superstitious New Englanders blamed vampires when people around them became pale, fatigued, coughed up blood, and slowly withered away. Concerned family members took matters into their own hands in hopes of curing their loved ones. In the simplest cases, suspected vampires were dug up and flipped upside down in their coffin, while other methods included breaking open the chest cavity to remove the heart, burning it, and then feeding the ashes to the afflicted.

Vampire exhumations might have been "clandestine, lantern-lit affairs" attended by a few family members, doctors, or clergy, or public and "festive" gatherings worthy of front-page newspaper stories, according to a *Smithsonian Magazine* article written by Abigail Tucker. Tucker retells a 1793 heart-burning ceremony in Manchester, New Hampshire, as described in the town's history: "Timothy Mead officiated at the altar in the sacrifice to the Demon Vampire who it was believed was still sucking the blood of the then-living wife of Captain Burton ... It was the month of February and good sleighing."

The last suspected vampire known to be unearthed in the United States was Mercy Lena Brown, a 19-year-old who died in Exeter, Rhode Island, in 1892. Mercy grew up in a farming family and was preceded in death by her mother, Mary, and her eldest sister, Mary Olive, both of whom died in 1883. Mercy and her brother Edwin contracted tuberculosis in 1891.

Though the much-feared disease was ravaging communities both large and small, the Brown family was particularly affected. In hopes of preserving the family bloodline, a dozen Browns convinced Mercy's father to unearth his wife and two daughters.

Mary and Mary Olive had died nearly a decade earlier and their bodies were found decomposed as expected. Mercy, however, had been dead for just two months and interred in an aboveground crypt for the winter. She was found in good condition with blood still in her heart and lungs. According to family lore, she had flipped over in her tomb (possible evidence that she had been buried alive though interpreted as another indicator of vampirism). Mercy was the Brown family's one and only vampire suspect. In hopes that Edwin would live, Mercy's heart and liver were torn out and burned right there in the cemetery, not too far from the family markers, as the local medical examiner looked on. Her ashes were mixed with water and given to her brother to drink. He died two months later. According to *Food for the Dead: On the Trail of New England's Vampires*, by the morning of March 19, 1892, the Brown family went nineteenth-century viral, with the front page of the *Providence Journal* declaring: "Bodies of Dead Relatives Taken From Their Graves."

According to New England historian Robert Bell, these appalling acts of digging up a family member and removing their organs and muscles were actually a sign of devotion in rural communities in the time before modern medicine; they were "an outward display that you are doing everything you can to fix the problem," as he told Tucker.

In *Vampires, Burial, and Death*, Paul Barber writes that vampiric practices were used throughout world history as a way for people to understand death, especially in ages and places where people didn't have access to sophisticated medical knowledge or research. "Our sources, in Europe as elsewhere, show a remarkable unanimity on this point: The dead may bring us death," Barber writes. "To prevent this we must lay them to rest properly, propitiate them, and, when all else fails, kill them a second time."

What was left of Mercy Brown's remains were buried in the family plot at the small Chestnut Hill Cemetery, which sits behind the Baptist Church of Exeter, just a few miles off Interstate 95. Her grave has become something of a dark tourist destination. In August 1996, the headstone disappeared and was mysteriously returned a week later. These days, a metal band holds the headstone in place and police keep an eye on the cemetery on Halloween. Vampire enthusiasts have been known to leave plastic fangs on the marker in solidarity, and in 2011, two Rhode Island teens died in a car crash after a trip to check out Brown's grave by moonlight.

REAL VAMPIRE CULTURE

Rod Ferrell and his friends, who spent their fair share of time in cemeteries, looked to the fictional and fringe "real vampire" culture that evolved out of punk and Goth culture in the 1970s.

According to researchers Megan White and Hatim Omar, "real vampire" behavior can include wearing prosthetic fangs, sleeping in a coffin, consuming blood, and only going outside at night, and the culture is believed to have evolved from role-playing games like Dungeons & Dragons and popular culture portrayals of the undead, such as Anne Rice's *Interview with the Vampire* and Stephenie Meyer's *Twilight* series.

These "real vampires" differ from clinical vampires, who believe they have a physical need to consume blood (and may get a sexual thrill from doing so). White and Omar write that "adolescents are naturally searching for identity and social bonding" and vampire cult activities, such as drinking blood, can serve as a way for otherwise disconnected teens to have intimate and empowering experiences. There's also the sexy and sensitive appeal of modern vampires, as portrayed in recent decades by Brad Pitt and Tom Cruise, but date back to the folkloric age when vampires were being disinterred, seemingly with erections (though this was likely just bloating in the nether regions from decomposing organs).

Rod Ferrell and his friends found community through their local vampire cult, which was believed to have about 30 to 40 members who engaged in group sex, drugs, and violent and ritualized cult behavior. Law-enforcement sources, as well as New York's Vampire Research Center, noted an increase in vampire activities after *Interview with a Vampire* hit movie theaters in 1994, and Ferrell also seemed to be inspired by the flick. According to an article in the *Independent* written by Daniel Jeffreys, Ferrell owed $30 in late fines for the movie rental, was caught surfing vampire material at his local library, and had pursued changing his name to Lestat after Rice's antihero.

Ferrell, who would later boast in interviews that his charisma helped him start a vampire cult, and whose grandfather believed he had the makings of a great spiritual leader, became an active member of Murray's vampire scene. A frequent hangout was the skeleton of a luxurious and long-abandoned lake house that the crew called the "Vampire Hotel." Locals, including Ferrell's own mother, gathered at the spot, which was littered with beer cans and spray-painted with occult symbols, to drink blood, perform rituals, and have sex by candlelight. Ferrell officially became a vampire with the help of then-best friend Steven Jaden Murphy, through a vampire initiation ceremony known as "crossing over." In a graveyard at night, Ferrell and Murphy drank each other's blood, with Murphy giving Ferrell a new, vampire name: Vesago.

Ferrell and future codefendant Howard Scott Anderson were also active in the Victorian Age Masquerade Performance Society, or VAMPS, a vampire role-playing group started in 1995 by a Murray State student named James Yohe. Eventually, Ferrell would become more interested in living as a vampire than pretending to be one. Yohe would later tell the *Ledger* that VAMPS was about improv, not blood-sucking. "People, no matter what, are always going to find a scapegoat and I don't want VAMPS to be that. We started out as a positive influence," Yohe told in the *Ledger*. (Shortly after the murders, *America's Most Wanted* warned parents of the dangers of vampire role-playing that could lead young people to the dark side.)

THE ROAD TO EUSTIS

Rod Ferrell was on law enforcement's radar for months before he drove to Florida and bashed in the Wendorfs' skulls. During the summer that led up to the murders, Ferrell's mother Sondra Gibson turned to Kentucky social services in hopes of getting her son—who had dropped out of school, was cutting himself, and using cocaine, heroin, and other hard drugs—back to reality (or at least a manageable state). Gibson told social workers that she'd seen Rod and his girlfriend drinking blood, and that Rod believed he was possessed. And Gibson had plenty of her own issues. In addition to her own satanic practices and trying to seduce boys who were her son's age, Gibson believed that demons had taken up residence outside her second-floor apartment window.

On November 25, the same day that Vampire Clan arrived in Eustis, Ferrell was supposed to stand before a Kentucky judge and explain why he hadn't written a two-page paper ordered by the court on the detrimental effects of drugs, the occult, and defiant behavior.

And then there were the animals. In October, Ferrell and another teen broke into the Murray-Calloway County Animal Shelter, torturing and killing two puppies, and beating 50 other dogs after letting them out of their kennels. They also trampled grass on the property in some sort of ritual act.

WKMS reporter John Null reported on what Sheriff Stan Scott said at the time: "We're dealing with some sick individuals and I want them caught. This goes way beyond a simple breaking and entering. One of these animals was stomped to death and the other had its legs either pulled or cut off. This is a case of absolute vandalism and these people need to be caught."

By early November, officials were preparing to arrest Ferrell and his accomplice on charges of animal cruelty and burglary.

After the Wendorf murders, others—including ex-best friend Murphy—recalled Ferrell being abusive toward animals, including one time when he hurled a cat against a tree, killing his pet in a fit of rage that seemingly came out of nowhere.

Researchers have long suspected a link between animal cruelty and criminal tendencies (serial killer Jeffrey Dahmer was fascinated with animal corpses from an early age). In their 2003 book, *Animal Cruelty: Pathway to Violence Against People*, University of South Florida professor Kathleen Heide and animal activist Linda Merz-Perez found in a study of 45 violent inmates in Florida prisons, half had abused animals when they were children. By comparison, 20 percent of non-violent criminals had participated in animal cruelty in their younger years.

"A lot of people who want to victimize, they want to start with something they can really control," Merz-Perez told the Associated Press. "The easiest thing in the world to control is a puppy. It's a matter of escalation, they work their way up."

Ferrell's mother, however, said there was no way he could have hurt all those dogs.

"Rod would never do that to an animal," Gibson told the *Orlando Sentinel* in 1998. "He had a little kitten that slept with him. He let that little kitten crawl all over him. He was at home asleep when that happened," she said, referring to the Murray-Calloway County Animal Shelter break-in and slaughter.

"I WANTED THEM ALIVE"

With Kentucky and the pending animal abuse charges in his rearview mirror, Ferrell set off with Howard Scott Anderson (vampire alias "Nosferatu"), Dana Cooper, who had frequented Murray's Vampire Hotel, and Charity Keesee, Ferrell's pregnant girlfriend.

The ride started out fun and upbeat, but the tension grew thicker as they continued south. Ferrell told the others that he had to pick up Wendorf, whom he referred to as "Zoey," before continuing on to New Orleans, a vampire-friendly city where "real vampires" lived together in communities and engaged in philanthropic activities, such as feeding the homeless, in addition to blood-drinking rituals.

The crew rolled into Eustis on Monday, November 25, three days before Thanksgiving, with Rod only giving Heather a 24-hour heads-up. The following day, she skipped her AP Art History class to meet Ferrell and his friends at Walmart to buy razors and then went to Greenwood Cemetery, just a few blocks away from Eustis High School.

At the cemetery, Ferrell started crossing over Heather. They both partook in ceremonial drinking of the others' blood, and according to Wendorf, Ferrell was her "sire."

"The person that gets crossed over is like subject to whatever the sire wants," Wendorf would later say in a deposition. "Like the sire is boss basically. They have authority over you."

The vampire cult also had to find a way to get Wendorf out of Eustis. One member offered up a possible scenario: Tie up Richard and Ruth and knock them unconscious, making it appear that Heather had been abducted.

"No, no!" Wendorf later told police was her response to that plan.

"I remember telling him flat out, 'Don't even go near my parents,' ... I wanted them alive," Wendorf claimed.

"ROD WENT CRAZY"

If you believe Rod Ferrell, he walked into 24135 Greentree Lane just planning to rob and hog-tie the Wendorfs—maybe rough them up a bit if they put up a fight—and then hit the road. If you believe the other teens swept up by Ferrell's "charisma," the self-proclaimed vampire king talked with Heather about his plan to take out the Wendorfs in the hours leading up to their murders.

No matter whose version you believe, Ferrell and Anderson entered the Wendorf residence through the garage, with Rod scooping up a crowbar before accessing the home through the unlocked garage door. Richard Wendorf, a 49-year-old manager at a metal manufacturing company, was asleep on the couch in front of a blaring television, his shoes kicked off. According to the *Orlando Sentinel*, the sound of running water let them know that Ruth Wendorf, a 54-year-old stay-at-home mother and school volunteer who loved crafting, gardening, and taking care of her chickens, was in the shower. And then, as Anderson would later put it, "Rod went crazy."

Fuck it, Ferrell thought, standing above his sleeping prey. He raised up the crowbar and brought it down on Richard Wendorf's face, neck, and chest more than 20 times, smashing his glasses and rendering his flesh the consistency of raw hamburger meat. Richard was pounded into his couch, with a thick blood stain forming on the cushions behind his head. After 20 agonizing minutes, Wendorf stopped shaking and succumbed to his injuries. A "v" mark was burned into his body, surrounded by circular marks that represented each member of Ferrell's clan.

Hearing the commotion, Ruth Wendorf came out of the shower, barefoot and dressed in a blue nightgown, and made her way to the kitchen, where she armed herself with a hot cup of coffee. When Ferrell appeared, Ruth lunged at her husband's murderer, dousing him with the scalding liquid and scratching his face with her fingernails. Ferrell later claimed that he was planning on letting Heather's mother live, but that her offensive maneuver sent him into a murderous rage.

"She clawed me, spilled fucking scalding hot coffee on me, pissed me off ... so I made sure she was dead," Rod later said in a confession to law enforcement.

Ferrell started hitting Ruth Wendorf repeatedly with the crowbar until he saw her brains coming out of a hole in the back of her head. The only consolation is that Ruth Wendorf did not suffer for as long as her husband—because her brain stem was severed, she likely died within a minute of Ferrell's attack.

All the while, Anderson looked on, though Ferrell claims he was an active accomplice who danced with him around Richard Wendorf as he slept on the couch. Before fleeing, Ferrell and Anderson collected a few possessions as requested by Heather, then slipped out of the now-silent home with the keys to the Explorer and Richard Wendorf's Discover Card.

Jennifer Wendorf, 17, was working late at her cashier job at Publix Super Markets while her parents were being murdered. The Eustis High cheerleader arrived home just after 10:30 p.m. and didn't look twice at her father, who appeared to have fallen asleep on the couch. As she turned the corner to grab a snack in the kitchen, Jennifer spotted a trail of blood. Then she saw her mother's body, facedown, the back of her skull bloody and gaping open. Jennifer ran back into the living room to rouse her father to get help. Only then did she realize that he wasn't asleep after all. The house phone had been ripped out of the wall, so she used her cell phone to call 911.

"I need two ambulances," Jennifer Wendorf told the dispatcher. "My mother and my father have just been killed. I just walked in the door. I don't know what happened. They are dead."

Jennifer had no idea if the assailants were still in the home but did know that two things were missing: her parents' blue 1993 Ford Explorer, and her younger sister Heather. Responding officers searched the Wendorf home with their guns drawn, turning up neither the attackers nor the teenager. No one knew if Heather was lying dead somewhere else, or kidnapped, or worse—a homicidal accomplice. A "Be on the Lookout" (BOLO) was issued for the Explorer, and a nationwide manhunt began.

HEADING WEST

Ferrell and Anderson ditched the Buick, swapping the license plates with the SUV (a critical error that would quickly link the Vampire Clan to the Wendorfs as soon as police ran the abandoned car's plates). Ferrell was still wearing a bloody T-shirt when he and Anderson picked up Heather and the girls and hit the road for Louisiana. Along the way, they burned their clothes and scrubbed their boots with steel wool pads in hopes of erasing all traces of the Wendorfs' blood. They hung on to the blood-caked murder weapon, using it to break into a house to steal $20 in change from a piggy bank for gas money that got them to Baton Rouge. Law enforcement believe the crowbar was eventually thrown into the Mississippi.

"The three days we were on the run, it was an utter rush. I loved that, because I knew every cop in the nation was looking for me," Ferrell recalled in the documentary *The Vampire Murders*, of those days on the lam. "The only hard part was keeping the other four in line."

Somewhere along the way, Heather learned that her parents had been killed. She later stated that she stayed with the group out of fear. If Ferrell took out her parents, what might he have had in store for her if she turned on him?

Back in Lake County, detectives were learning more about Rod Ferrell from Jeanine Leclair, another one of his ex-girlfriends who had been planning to run away with them but was stopped by her mother.

Charity Keesee was the first to crack and call her family. The calls helped Kentucky and Louisiana law enforcement narrow down their location and track the clan down at a Howard Johnson's hotel. Officers were waiting when the Ford Explorer, driven by Heather Wendorf, pulled into the motel parking lot on Thanksgiving Day morning.

If responding officer James Welbourne didn't know who was running the show before, it was clear from his first encounter who was boss of the teens.

"From my observations, Ferrell appeared to be the one in control, the one the others looked to for guidance because they were scared. In fact, Rod Ferrell was intimidating—that was one reason I called for backup," he was reported to say in the book *Blood and Lust*.

The other four teens were cooperative and subdued. The group was separated, Ferrell and Anderson in the back of one patrol car and Wendorf, Cooper, and Keesee in the other.

Back at the station, there was legal red tape to cut before law enforcement could question the suspects. State law in Louisiana mandates that a parent or guardian be present when a minor is questioned, which is not required in Florida. After a call to Lake County, where a state attorney assured them that Florida had jurisdiction, Ferrell was read his Miranda rights and Louisiana detectives start asking him what happened back in Eustis. Over several hours, Ferrell told detectives that he was the guardian of the Kentucky Vampire Clan, and that he was first introduced to vampirism by his grandfather, witnessing a sacrifice when he was just six years old. (Harrell Gibson, Ferrell's grandfather, would later deny these claims in an *Orlando Sentinel* article, calling upon his Pentecostal faith. "There hasn't been any drinking, tobacco, or abusive language in our house since 1958," Gibson said. "If there was vampirism, it wasn't going on in our house.")

Ferrell told detectives that "if you take a life, you become a god for a split second. I actually kind of felt that way for a minute." In a 1999 appeal, Ferrell and his attorneys said this was a "tainted confession" pulled out of a sleep-deprived teen who only wanted to see his pregnant girlfriend.

LEADING UP TO TRIAL

The Vampire Clan was extradited back to Florida. On December 16, 1996, Anderson, Cooper, and Keesee were indicted by a grand jury on charges of principal to first-degree murder, armed robbery, and armed burglary. The following day, Rod Ferrell was hit with a first-degree murder indictment and pleaded not guilty. Heather Wendorf was released from a juvenile center after a grand jury cleared her of any involvement in her parents' death, though an unsealed affidavit would later reveal that Heather had asked her sister Jennifer if she had ever thought of killing their parents, and, if she wanted someone killed, Rod Ferrell would be the person for the job.

Ferrell and the teen codefendants remained in the media spotlight for years. But the main cast, as well as the supporting characters, didn't make it easy for them to fade into morbid obscurity.

Ferrell was a cocky showman in court hearings, flicking his tongue at news cameras, kissing the glass door panels, and boasting to guards that they were too stupid to prevent him from taking hostages and busting out of jail. Anderson was received as a celebrity at the Lake County Jail, with inmates gathering outside his cell door when he first arrived. But his vampire antics, which included sitting crouched in a gargoyle stance for hours and gnawing on the bars, wore on his former fans, who took to throwing cold water on Anderson while he slept. Charity Keesee and another woman were caught "licking or kissing" blood out of cuts inflicted by a Bic razor. Back in Kentucky, Ferrell's mother was arrested after sending "lurid" letters to a 14-year-old that she wanted to cross her over.

"I longed to be near you, for your embrace. Yes ... to become a vampire, a part of the family, immortal and truly yours forever," Gibson wrote in the note, which her lawyer unsuccessfully argued was protected speech. Gibson was spared the maximum sentence of a decade in prison for the felony, pleading guilty but mentally ill to first-degree criminal attempt to commit an unlawful transaction with a minor. She received probation and was mandated by the court to attend counseling.

DODGING "OL' SPARKY"

With jurors selected and his trial set to begin, Ferrell had an unexpected announcement to make in court: He was going to plead guilty to the murders. Since Ferrell was facing the death penalty, the 12 jurors were still tasked with deciding if he would get life in prison or die for his crimes during the penalty phase of the trial.

During proceedings, it was established that Ferrell was under extreme mental and physical distress when he killed the Wendorfs, possibly taking up to eight hits of LSD that day. Two defense psychologists testified that Ferrell came from an extremely dysfunctional family and that he had schizotypal personality disorder, which usually leads to odd or eccentric behavior, the inability to cultivate close relationships, and difficulty understanding how personal behavior might affect others. Ferrell had a lifetime of "pent-up rage spurred by a dysfunctional family that did not provide him with the emotional support he needed," and had confused fantasy with reality, said psychologist Elizabeth McMahon. Despite Ferrell not showing any remorse for the murders, McMahon told the court that he might have a chance to be rehabilitated if he were to live in a structured environment.

According to State Attorney Brad King, Ferrell wasn't *so* out of his mind: He was capable enough to sneak into the Wendorfs' home after almost mistakenly entering a neighbors' house, switch the license plates, and get rid of the crowbar.

After deliberating, the jurors unanimously agreed that Rod Ferrell should die for the murders of Richard and Ruth Wendorf. Age 17 at the time of the crime, he is the youngest person sentenced to "Ol' Sparky," the nickname given to Florida's electric chair. After Ol' Sparky was blamed for several less-than-seamless executions in the 1990s, including a prisoner's face mask catching on fire and flames shooting out of another man's head, the electric chair was retired in favor of lethal injection. Ol' Sparky still remains an option for Florida inmates, and death row inmate Wayne Doty, who was sentenced to death after he strangled and repeatedly stabbed a fellow inmate at Florida State Prison, was the first to express his preference to die by electrocution in 2015. (He remains on death row.)

"I think you are a disturbed young man. I think your family failed you. I think society failed you," Circuit Judge Jerry Lockett said at the sentencing, adding that Ferrell's mother ought to face charges as well. Lockett also asked state prosecutors to convene a second grand jury to look at new evidence against Heather Wendorf.

Ferrell didn't seem to mind being on death row. In a prison interview, he romantically reflected on his future execution, saying that it had always been a dream of his to get the electric chair, and that he had been fantasizing about his own death since he was 9 years old.

Even though he told the court that he "froze" during the slayings and was a fearful onlooker, not a participant, Anderson took a plea deal and was sentenced to two consecutive life terms without parole.

"This is a lot better than what Ferrell got," Anderson told *Orlando Sentinel* reporter Frank Stanfield.

In fact, none of the codefendants went to trial. Dana Cooper, the only adult at the time of the murders and Louisiana joyride, pleaded guilty to charges of principal to third-degree murder, armed robbery, and armed burglary, and was sentenced to 17½ years in prison. Final codefendant Charity Keesee also took a deal and was sentenced to 10½ years in prison in August 1998.

In December 1998, two years after the teens had been arrested in Baton Rouge, a second grand jury was convened to decide whether or not Heather Wendorf should stand for charges related to her parents' murders. Even though the local sheriff, circuit judge, and others were convinced she was involved, as well as a pair of witnesses who testified that Wendorf had talked about wanting her parents dead, she was cleared a second time. For what his word is worth, Ferrell (and his family) maintain that Heather ordered the murders. And Ferrell told daytime talk show host Maury Povich—but not the grand jury—that Wendorf was to blame for the whole thing.

In an opinion piece that ran in the *Orlando Sentinel* a year before the second grand jury's findings, staff writer Ramsey Campbell argued that Ferrell was far easier to convict than Wendorf.

"How could she be a member of this vampire cult, run away with them the night of the murders, and not be charged with something?" Campbell wrote. "The answer is simple. She was inconvenient to the prosecution. It would be hard to convince any jury—especially in the South—that a white middle-class girl of 16 would be capable of participating—even indirectly— in her parents' killings."

THE VAMPIRE CLAN TODAY

In 2000, the Florida Supreme Court commuted Ferrell's death sentence to life in prison after ruling that a defendant must be 17 or older at the time of the offense to be eligible for capital punishment. There is a chance that both Ferrell and Anderson will walk out of prison one day, as their cases will be reheard by a judge in 2018 for possible resentencing.

Ferrell's mother Sondra Gibson now goes by "Star." She lives in central Florida and is optimistic about Rod Ferrell's prospects of a reduced sentence.

Charity Keesee was released from prison in March 2006 and Dana Cooper got out in October 2011. Prison release records show that both women returned to their hometown of Murray, Kentucky.

Though legally in the clear, Heather Wendorf's family relationships were strained following the murders. She fell out with her grandmother, Gertrude Adams, after the elder woman fired a pistol in the air to get Wendorf to stop screaming. Things didn't improve, especially after Wendorf signed an exclusive deal to tell her story to true crime writer Aphrodite Jones. Heather completed high school while living with one of her attorneys, who was appointed her foster parent, and went on to study at the North Carolina School of the Arts.

In 2006, Wendorf was still living in North Carolina and had recently married a film director. She remained distant from her family and friends but had reconnected with many family members when she attended her grandmother's funeral three years earlier. She reflected on her childhood as "almost perfect" and her fleeting interest in vampirism as "something special in your life that you felt secret about."

Still, the weight of her past weighs on:

"It's hard not to feel guilty when every news station in America is telling you you're guilty," Wendorf told the *Orlando Sentinel*.

CHAPTER 9

HEAVEN'S GATE

It was a beautiful Wednesday afternoon in southern California. The year was 1997. Encinitas Sheriff's Deputy Robert Brunk, 35, had reported to his afternoon shift at the San Diego County Sheriff's Department expecting to field vehicle break-ins, assist lifeguard calls, and disband drunken scuffles—the usual duties for a patrol cop in a beach town. But that day, he was told to call the dispatch center.

A woman on the other end of the line said they had received an anonymous 911 call about two hours earlier reporting that a religious group had committed mass suicide. Brunk was being sent up to Rancho Santa Fe, about 25 miles north of downtown San Diego and one of the highest income areas of the United States, to check it out.

Brunk and the operator had a laugh about the call before he left. *Probably just a prank,* he told himself on the 10-minute ride to 18241 Colina Norte, a two-story gilded Mediterranean-style mansion in a gated community. Along the way, he rehearsed the words he'd use to explain to the home's residents who swung open the mansion's heavy double doors that he was there to investigate a tip that dozens of "Cultifornians" had reportedly offed themselves inside.

Brunk pulled his cruiser up in front of the house. The mansion's gate was locked—the first sign that something was up—so he hopped it. Walking up the driveway, the officer with three years of patrol experience under his belt felt unease rise up from the bottom of his gut. He could see that the curtains were drawn and the lights were on inside the 9,200-square-foot mansion. Air conditioners were running. Multiple vehicles in the garage and driveway came back as unregistered to the mansion's owner. Brunk knocked at the front door—nothing. Around the side, he found an unlocked door. He knocked—again no answer—and opened the door. "Sheriff's Office!," he announced, and he was met with the unmistakable smell of death inside the home.

Brunk's training kicked in—he knew better than to go into a house that reeked of dead bodies without backup. About 10 minutes later, Sheriff's Deputy Laura Gacek was on the scene. With their guns drawn and dispatchers aware of their movements, they entered the home. They saw the bodies around the same time, lying on bunk beds, a mattress on the floor, and a collapsible table. Not knowing what could have killed these people and suspecting that poisonous fumes could be in the air, Brunk and Gacek fled the house.

"Tell Omega I lost count at 10," Brunk radioed back to dispatch once safely outside the mansion, referring to the police radio code for the coroner.

But there were many more than 10 bodies, nearly four times that, in fact. Over the course of that late afternoon on March 26, 1997, investigators would find 39 bodies in various stages of decomposition. Cropped haircuts led investigators to initially believe that all 39 were men, but autopsies later revealed that 21 women and 18 men had died there. As if this discovery wasn't shocking enough, eight of the men had been castrated.

There was another peculiarity about the scene: Everyone was wearing the same loose, black clothing. A triangle patch sewed onto the left shoulder that depicted the Orion constellation read "Heaven's Gate Away Team." Everything was uniform—the squeaky clean, brand-new Nike sneakers, the $5 bill and three quarters in their pockets, the packed duffel bag next to the bed.

They wore gold bands on their left ring finger and tucked passports or birth certificates in their shirt pockets. Eyeglasses were properly folded and placed next to their hands, in reach just in case they ever woke up again. Thirty-seven of the bodies were covered with a purple shroud, all except those who would later be determined to be the last two cult members to take their own lives with a deadly mix of applesauce or pudding cut with phenobarbital, an anti-seizure medication, washed down with vodka and aided in asphyxiation by a plastic bag. The cult's leader, Marshall Applewhite, who was known as "Do" to his followers, was found dead in the master bedroom.

Computer screens in the house displayed heavensgate.com, the group's website, with RED ALERT flashing in capital letters and bold red text at the top of the screen. That afternoon, the bodies were removed from the home on stretchers, their purple shrouds swapped out for white body bags and stacked into an awaiting refrigerated coroner's truck. Meanwhile, investigators were learning more about this group that called themselves Heaven's Gate, and why they decided to take their own lives.

The cultists had spent 22 years studying with Applewhite and training to enter the kingdom of heaven with him. To reach this extraterrestrial realm, they would have to shed their earthly bodies. After decades of strict communal living and preparation, they found the omen that they were looking for— the Hale-Bopp comet, discovered two years earlier in the skies above the Southwest, now visible to the naked eye. Heaven's Gate believed that a spaceship tailed this comet, and that the suicides would transport the members to that awaiting spacecraft. Once on board, they'd be reunited with Bonnie Lu Nettles, or "Ti," who cofounded Heaven's Gate with Applewhite in the early 1970s and had died from cancer more than a decade earlier.

Video tapes mailed to CNN and *60 Minutes* confirmed this seemingly unbelievable notion, that these 39 people voluntarily killed themselves to ascend to an "evolutionary level above human."

Within hours, hundreds of reporters were on the scene outside 18241 Colina Norte, waiting for more updates on the largest mass suicide to ever happen on American soil.

The people who decided to follow Do and Ti around the country were young, old, and in-between, ranging in age from 26 to 72, living a nomadic and monastic lifestyle and learning the teachings, which had roots in evangelical Christianity, science fiction, and the New Age movement of alternative religions that were very much an extension of 1960s counterculture. They came from Florida, Missouri, New Hampshire, Canada. Before the cult, they had been graphic designers and computer developers, CEOs turned environmentalists, bus drivers, musicians, parents. One woman had joined just months before their mass suicide in March 1997, while others had been with the group for decades. Above all they were spiritual seekers who were contemplating the meaning of why we're on this planet—and beyond.

> *There is no place for us here. It is time for us to go home—to God's Kingdom, to the Next Level. There is no place for us to go but up.*
>
> —Glnody, a Heaven's Gate student

THE TWO

Before there was Heaven's Gate, before the 39 suicides, before there was Do and Ti, there was Marshall Herff Applewhite and Bonnie Lu Nettles.

Applewhite, known as "Herff" before he became "Do," was born in 1931 in Spur, Texas. He was the son of a Presbyterian minister who uprooted the family every few years to establish new churches around South Texas. Applewhite had three siblings, a passion for music, and the ambition to follow in his father's footsteps. While studying philosophy at Austin College, Applewhite pursued both of these callings, leading extracurricular groups for aspiring Presbyterian ministers, and singing in an a capella group. In *Heaven's Gate: America's UFO Religion*, one classmate recalled Heaven's Gate future leader as an extrovert who was bound to use his talents for good in the world.

After graduation, Applewhite studied at Virginia's Union Theological Seminary for a semester before dropping out to pursue music, taking a choir director job in Gastonia, North Carolina. An Army stint relocated Applewhite and his then-wife, Ann Pearce, to Salzburg, Austria, in 1954, followed by White Sands, New Mexico, where Applewhite served in the Army Signal Corps as an instructor and later owned the Sunshine Company deli in Taos.

He had two children whom he was "deeply devoted to," according to his sister. And with his young family in tow, Applewhite crisscrossed the United States for music-related positions. He eventually earned his master's degree in music and voice from the University of Colorado, where he landed the lead in the musical productions of *South Pacific* and *Oklahoma!* and made his way back to Texas, where he worked in churches and synagogues and taught in the fine arts program at the University of St. Thomas in Houston.

Applewhite and his wife separated in the mid-1960s and were divorced by the end of the decade. (He reportedly never saw his wife or his children again.) Following the suicides in Rancho Santa Fe, much media attention was devoted to Applewhite's sexuality and the cult's rigid views that required members to give up sex and leave behind their partners and children. In an April 1997 profile on Heaven's Gate in the *New York Times*, writer Barry Bearak described Applewhite as a sexual chameleon seen in some social circles as a "dashing man about town" who was always accompanied by a "well-off, well-dressed woman." In other settings, Applewhite was a gay man who lived with his "longtime lover" in Houston's LGBT-friendly Montrose neighborhood.

In a documentary interview, *Heaven's Gate: Inside Story*, conducted shortly after the suicides, musician and former member Michael Conyers said that Do's Christian upbringing, coupled with the attitude at the time that homosexuality was a mental illness, fueled his belief that the body was "abhorrent."

"He didn't like his homosexuality, he was hiding from a piece of himself that he disliked. So he created a myth around that piece that he didn't like," Conyers said.

By some accounts, it was an affair with a male student that led Applewhite to resign from his teaching position at the University of St. Thomas in 1970, citing emotional health issues, and into the platonically comfortable arms of Bonnie Lu Nettles.

Depending on whom you ask—or whom you believe—Applewhite met Nettles in the psychiatric ward of a Houston hospital in March 1972. Perhaps he was just at the hospital visiting a sick friend. Or maybe he was being hospitalized after a heart blockage that nearly killed him. Perhaps they didn't meet at the hospital at all, but an acting school. Whether he was committed or not, Applewhite was mentally unraveling leading up to the time of his supposed hospitalization, and took an interest in UFOs, science fiction, astrology, and mysticism prior to meeting Nettles. But his Heaven's Gate cofounder, who would later take on the name Ti, was way ahead of the spiritual game.

Raised as a Baptist, Nettles developed an interest in the occult and started holding weekly séances in her living room for a group of like-minded seekers. They made contact with a nineteenth-century monk known as "Brother Francis," as well as more glamorous encounters, such as Marilyn Monroe. Nettles' New Age enthusiasm eventually led to a divorce from her husband, who didn't share her excitement in encountering the undead.

After they were introduced, Applewhite and Nettles were immediately inseparable, and Nettles provided a nurturing spiritual base for Applewhite, who often had a hard time putting his religious experiences into words. After swiftly opening and closing both a bookstore and retreat center in the Houston area, Applewhite and Nettles hit the open road on New Year's Day, driving thousands of miles a month across the United States, up to Canada and back, subsisting at times on only bread and butter and gobbling up spiritual books from different traditions. That summer, their spiritual destiny became clear to them while camping on the banks of Oregon's Rogue River. They were the two witnesses from the New Testament Book of Revelations destined to be martyred by the Antichrist. They knew the way to enter the kingdom of heaven, the level above human. All they needed was some followers to show the way.

ASSEMBLING THE CLASS

God has sent us here as an experiment, so you might call us Guinea and Pig.

—Marshall Applewhite at a Los Angeles meeting

With a clear vision, Do and Ti were ready to start growing their flock, whom they would later refer to as "the class." They found their first convert in Sharon Morgan, a seeker who was unhappy with her marriage, and who, within six days of meeting Applewhite and Nettles, left her husband and two-year-old daughter behind in Texas to spread the word. Applewhite and Nettles spent the summer of 1974 road-tripping and proselytizing with their new convert. The trio would skip out on food and hotel bills and using the Morgan family credit card for the purchases they did pay. Morgan was forced back to conventional life about four months later, when a stop in Dallas turned into a family intervention. (But her connection to Heaven's Gate didn't end there. In a *New York Times* story following the mass suicide, Morgan, by then a 53-year-old stockbroker who went by the last name Walsh, told the paper that her half-sister, Judith Ann Rowland, died with the cult, and that her mother, stepfather, and niece were members as well.)

Police didn't move forward with any charges stemmed to John Morgan's complaint, but a warrant check linked Applewhite to a stolen rental car out of Missouri—fittingly, a Mercury Comet—that he was still tooling around in. Applewhite spent the next six months in jail where he further refined the Heaven's Gate mission to include the idea that he and Nettles were extraterrestrials housed in human bodies, just waiting for their opportunity to ascend to the next level. Heaven's Gate theology would change over the next two decades, particularly after Nettles' death, but this ET connection would remain a core tenet of the group.

Though they couldn't keep Sharon Morgan around, two major recruiting events in the mid-1970s would significantly increase the number of Do and Ti followers. Their first brush with guru stardom took place in 1975 in the Studio City home of Joan Culpepper, a meditation teacher, spiritual counselor, and recently laid-off advertising executive with a personal motto: "Weird turns me on." Her friend, Clarence Klug, had recently met Applewhite and Nettles in Ojai, and helped arrange a gathering of about 80 people at Culpepper's apartment to hear about UFO teachings from the The Two and their Human Individual Metamorphosis group, as Heaven's Gate was known back then. The Two showed up in sweat suits and desert boots, according to Culpepper's account in the *LA Times* nearly two decades later.

"They were very stern," Culpepper recalled. "There was not any kind of loving kindness or nurturing. They said they would die, be assassinated, and anyone who followed would travel with them on a spaceship to a higher level, to heaven."

A *New York Times* profile expanded on The Two's rigidity, recreating Applewhite's rhetoric from that LA gathering: "If you follow, then you must obey everything we say. That includes giving up your possessions, your family, and your entire identity." This was not a typical, sugar-coated cult recruitment.

Culpepper wasn't convinced by Applewhite, she reportedly addressed him as "Mr. Pig" that evening and asked him questions laced with sarcasm. But anywhere from two dozen to a third of the 80 attendees were smitten, and left that night to follow Applewhite and Nettles north to the Oregon Coast, in search of more recruits. (Culpepper felt responsible for setting the whole thing up and spent the years to come speaking out against the cult, attending Heaven's Gate appearances to stare down Applewhite, and housing former members at a halfway house in Topanga Canyon.)

Later that fall, Applewhite and Nettles would make the national news after a large gathering in Waldport, Oregon, led to dozens of people walking out on their lives to join the group. According to *Oregon Live*, posters announcing their appearance read: "UFOs. Why they are here. Who they have come for. When they will leave." Their appearance drew a crowd that ranged from 100 to more than 250, according to conflicting newspaper reports, and an estimated 20 to 33 people joining up.

The disappearances did not go unnoticed. Walter Cronkite, the legendary CBS News anchor and reporter, announced during a nightly broadcast that "a score of persons from a small Oregon town have disappeared. It's a mystery whether they've been taken on a so-called trip to eternity—or simply been taken."

Although Heaven's Gate was more popular than ever in the late seventies—ballooning to some 200 members during those years—the leaders felt mocked and "shot down by the media," according to a 1988 cult document made public by the *Washington Post*, and this heat sent the cultists underground. No one could find Applewhite and Nettles. The group physically dispersed as well, communicating through post office boxes and covert phone messages. Some members started smoking pot openly and questioned if Applewhite and Nettles were who they said they were, according to accounts by the infiltrator sociologist Robert Balch.

In April 1976, Nettles announced that "the harvest is closed"; no more recruits allowed. A few months later, about a hundred followers gathered at Medicine Bow National Forest in Wyoming, where The Two outlined their plan to create the Human Individual Metamorphosis community, which included strict bans on sex and drug use.

In *Heaven's Gate: Postmodernity and Pop Culture in a Suicide Group*, religious scholar George Chryssides describes the tough-love crackdown from The Two:

> *Ti and Do announced that it had been rumored that some were still occasionally indulging in pot and sex. Everyone was asked to go off by themselves for a few hours and make up their mind as to whether they were just caught up in the fun of a "movement" or if they were serious. For now the real "classroom" was to begin, and it was not for those who felt they wanted to hold on to human ways. Ti and Do preached long and hard about what it meant to rid oneself of self, and what would be required of those who continued.*

Membership dropped to 80 in the coming days, then to 70 when the winter storms started rolling through in October. The butter had been clarified, Nettles put it, the pure had been separated from the impure. The Two had their class.

In retrospect, UFOs seem far out, but not so in the 1970s New Age movement, which took an interest in flying saucers in addition to reincarnation and cosmic consciousness. The UFO phenomenon emerged in the 1940s, coinciding with the rise of Cold War tensions, and the CIA actively investigated unidentified flying objects for the next two decades. The results of a 1973 Gallup poll found that 95 percent Americans were familiar with the concept of UFOs, and 57 percent of those polled believed that UFOs were real (Presidents Jimmy Carter and Ronald Reagan were also believers).

Conyers, who joined the cult in 1975, said he was initially attracted to the group because Applewhite and Nettles brought a scientifically relevant update to his Christian upbringing.

"Mary was impregnated by being taken up on a spacecraft. Now as unbelievable as that sounds, that was an answer that was better than the plain virgin birth," Conyers said in *Heaven's Gate: Inside Story*.

Cult expert Janja Lalich had written that the appeal of Heaven's Gate was that Applewhite and Nettles were "offering something different—something unique, yet familiar" by taking New Age concepts to the next level.

"This was not the same old trip with the best hit of acid or some old long-haired group sprouting the same old verses out of the same old Bible or Hindu text. What these two were offering seemed to be better, combining a little bit of everything and it came across as really 'far out,'" Lalich wrote in a 2004 article for *Cultic Studies Review*. "These two prophets and their newly gathered disciples sounded knowledgeable enough and mysterious enough to entice the curious and the sincere."

LIFE IN HEAVEN'S GATE

With the freeloaders and stoners weeded out, Applewhite and Nettles started acting more like cult leaders, controlling the social and religious lives of their class.

From the late 1970s through the mass suicide, the cult lived mostly underground, reemerging only a handful of times over the next 20 years for public appearances. They were nomadic, moving around frequently and living in rented houses or campgrounds that were paid for, in part, from a member's trust fund. One of their endeavors included a half-built "earth ship" on 40 acres near New Mexico's Manzano Mountains that they later abandoned. At times, they also lived in public parks and begged for food.

In their book *Cults in Our Midst*, Margaret Singer and Janja Lalich write that "if you really want to change people, change their appearance ... cult members can be asked or told to cut their hair or wear it in a particular style, wear different clothes, take on new names, and assume certain gestures of mannerisms."

Singer and Lalich weren't specifically talking about Heaven's Gate, though the cult employed most, if not all, of these tactics. Heaven's Gate wore formless clothing (Do and Ti reportedly favored TJ Maxx and Burlington Coat Factory for the cult's clothes, which were all shared communally, down to the underwear). Heaven's Gate was aspiring to reach a higher level that they believed was genderless. All members had the same short haircut, and women shunned makeup, dresses, and any other attributes that might show off their feminine, human form in hopes of quashing any sexual desire or prowess.

Lalich later noted in *Cultic Studies Review* that "at the extreme, a feeling of self-hate was instilled in Heaven's Gate members, reframed as a hatred of their human self, known as the 'vehicle' in their parlance. This likely stemmed from Applewhite's attitudes toward his own sexuality," and "evidently struggling with one's vehicle was a requirement, and a daily reality." Life on Earth was a "torturous ... training ground" for the next level, and any human act was seen as a detriment to them ascending to the level above human.

One former member recalled that even though no one was having sex, that's all anyone ever seemed to talk about. In an effort to curb desire, each Heaven's Gate member was assigned a "check partner" to keep each other accountable in terms of sexuality and any other activity (according to Heaven's Gate rules, taking "any action" without one's check partner was a "lesser" offense"). Members were advised to report any sexual fantasies, or slippages, to Do. A slippage meant that there was more work to do to advance to the next level of consciousness.

To cut future cravings off at the pass, some male members of Heaven's Gate started thinking about going directly to the source of the issue: their testicles.

Applewhite's students asked for years about the possibility of castrating themselves to relieve their sexual urges. In 1993, Steven McCarter became the first to undergo the procedure after "winning" a coin toss against another cult member called Sawyer who was also hoping to undergo the procedure. The group wasn't able to find a doctor willing to perform the castration stateside, so McCarter had to travel to Mexico for the simple operation, which nonetheless was botched by the surgeon's assistant (and subsequently led his scrotum to heavily swell due to improper drainage). Still, seven more Heaven's Gate members, including Applewhite, went under the knife.

While castration was voluntary, all other aspects of life in Heaven's Gate were by the book, literally, the "Procedures Book." The cult had rigid rules for just about everything. Only certain cultists were allowed outside of their rented homes in an effort to not draw attention to the group and make it appear as if fewer people were living there. Class members were assigned seating in front of the 72-inch television. The Procedures Book even outlined the correct way for men to shave their face (down, not up), the appropriate shower length (six minutes), and the amount of water to be used (one gallon). Even the size of their pancakes and the amount of coffee brewed for their frequent enemas, one of the many dietary tactics used for physical and spiritual purging, were regulated. All purchases were noted in a financial ledger that kept a tally of rent payments, grocery lists, library fines, even an event during which two members found 6 cents. All this structure was in preparation for the discipline that they'd need as crew members on a spaceship.

Heaven's Gate even had their own language to help them reach the next level of consciousness. Breakfast was known as the "first experiment," Rio DiAngelo, a former Heaven's Gate member, writes in his 2007 self-published book, *Beyond Human Mind.* The first experiment was followed, naturally, by a second and third throughout the day. Recipes were called "formulas"; their office was a "compulab." Perhaps most puzzling is a bra, known to the cultists as a "sling shot."

Like many cults, Heaven's Gate created an environment where members had to walk away from their family, possessions, and identities, and could not freely come and go as they pleased. Members were given new names that included a variation of -ODY at the end. Any contact with parents or other family members were initiated by Heaven's Gate members, not the other way around. As the group matured, many members went from working entry-level jobs to jobs in their areas of expertise (always secured using fake resumes and references), including web design. According to reporter Barry Bearak, the cult was bringing in around $400,000 a year after taxes.

According to Michael Conyers, cult members stayed because of idle threats and fear of not being included when it came time to ascend to the next level. "What ended up happening was there were these idle threats, from my point of view, of fear, that if you missed the boat, you may not get another chance."

In an interview for *Cults that Kill*, Lalich said her theory of "bounded choice" explains why the Heaven's Gate cultists stayed. The idea, Lalich says, is that as you get more involved with the cult and start abiding by their rules and start to internalize their beliefs, you hold yourself accountable to stay loyal to the group or leader and follow the expected guidelines and orders. At this point, the group becomes your life; you don't have any outside ideas or influences.

"[When] you enter into this state of mind that I call 'bounded choice,' which means that any decision that you have to make, you know exactly what your choice is in order to remain in good favor of the group. And the thought of leaving the group equals death, either real or metaphorical," Lalich said.

"So you're totally, in a sense, paralyzed by fear of taking any other action, and you make the decision that the cult wants you to make that you yourself want to make. This whole issue revolves around free will and whether or not people have free will, and people in that video were saying I'm doing this of my own free will. So what this is is an illusion of choice, that your free will has actually been altered by the will of the group. So yes, nobody's holding a gun to your head, but they may as well be, because you know the choice that you have to make."

THE FINAL EXIT

We're so excited we don't know what we're going to do.
—Marshall Applewhite

Throughout history, a comet appearing in the sky above Earth has been a cause for concern. Comets were bad omens in the Middle Ages, and have been blamed for fires, wars, the fall of the Alamo, William the Conqueror's invasion of England—even the life and death of Mark Twain, who was born two weeks after Halley's Comet was visible in 1835 and died one day after the comet passed by again in 1910. In 1908, poisonous gas had been detected on the tail of Comet Morehouse, so when Halley rolled back through, women plugged up the windows and doors of their home in hopes of keeping out toxic fumes. A Haitian voodoo doctor and two hawkers in Texas reportedly sold "comet pills"—a combination of sugar and quinine—to ward off any side effects of the comet's supposedly noxious tail.

But when the Hale-Bopp comet, estimated to be three to four times bigger than Halley's Comet and a thousand times brighter, appeared to two astronomers, Alan Hale and Thomas Bopp, in the summer of 1995, Heaven's Gate turned toward the discovery with excitement, not fear. They bought a telescope and took turns watching the body of frozen gases, rock, and dust.

A decade earlier, Heaven's Gate cofounder Bonnie Lu Nettles had died from cancer in a Dallas hospital, where she had been admitted under the pseudonym Shelly West. Her ashes were spread in a Texas lake, and the core of Heaven's Gate theology was rocked. Though Heaven's Gate was opposed to suicide in theory (a web page on their website is devoted to this topic), Applewhite distanced himself from the idea that you could ascend to the next level while still in your earthly body. Now, he taught the class, you had to leave your vehicle to reach the next level of consciousness.

In Hale-Bopp they had a sign from Ti that the time had come to shed their husks and join her in the next level. With the comet visible to the naked eye, Heaven's Gate made their final preparations. They started filming "exit statements," taped video messages that outlined their reasons for leaving this world and convincing the rest of us that this was their choice. The videos, available on YouTube, show members of the class against a sunny, southern California backdrop, complete with birds chirping. Some are stern, others are smiling, laughing nervously when the videographer announces that the camera is now rolling.

One cultist named Lvvody said she was one of those who disappeared from Waldport, Oregon. Wearing a shapeless, plaid shirt, she quickly chokes up when describing the pride she felt as a student of Applewhite and Nettles and her happiness about their planned exit.

"Doubt was never an issue," Lvvody said. "There's always a deep-down knowing, that from the moment of seeing Ti and Do, that this is why I'm here, to take this vehicle and do this task."

Another member called Dstody said he joined the class in March 1976 during a time where he was searching for meaning in life. "I don't know what I did to deserve to be here," Dstody says with a slight hint of a southern accent. "I'm the happiest person in the world."

The Heaven's Gate members express their appreciation to Do and Ti for their patience as the class worked through their human inclinations. They also anticipate how the media is going to depict Do and Ti, and say that they are taking their lives on their own terms.

"I'm going to shed this husk, it's worthless, it's useless to me," says Tllody, who wears a navy button-down shirt and explains that his impending poisoning and asphyxiation is no different than a chrysalis shedding its cocoon. He continues:

> The bottom line is I am doing this of my own free will, I have chosen to do it, it's not something that somebody brainwashed me into or convinced me of or did a con job on, it's something I have grown to know and understand and of my own will have chosen to do .... This planet has become a hideous, hideous place, they take control of you from the cradle to the grave, you have no choices unless the next level offers you choices, and most of the time you're herded around like animals.

For their last supper, Heaven's Gate traveled up to Carlsbad to dine at Marie Callender's. They all shared the same meal at the chain restaurant: iced teas with lots of lemon, salad with a tomato vinegar dressing, turkey pot pie for their main course, and cheesecake with blueberries on top for dessert. The purchases were noted in their ledger, and their server recalled the bunch as upbeat, polite, and decidedly not depressed.

Had the final exit happened a few weeks earlier, cult member Rio DiAngelo might have been among the dead. Just weeks before the suicides, DiAngelo approached Do with a premonition that he had a different role to play in the cult.

"I had this feeling that was the same feeling that I had when I joined, it was kind of an irresistible feeling that my focus, or my task, was different," said DiAngelo, who first encountered the group in 1988. "I felt like I had a task to do outside of the class for the class in some way that I did not understand." As reported in *Heaven's Gate: Inside Story*, after an emotional conversation, Applewhite told DiAngelo that his leaving was probably part of the design, and he left the cult, going to work for InterAct Entertainment Company in Beverly Hills.

On March 26, 1997, DiAngelo received the exit tapes via Federal Express, as well as a note that outlined the suicides and what door to enter the mansion. The following day DiAngelo hitched a ride from his boss, Nick Matzorkis, and together they made the nearly three-hour drive south to Rancho Santa Fe. At 18241 Colina Norte, DiAngelo entered the same side door that investigators would find unlocked hours later, smelled the same scents of decomposition, and called out to see if anyone was still alive. No one answered.

"And so I walked around the house videotaping things, because I wanted to make sure that this was portrayed accurately," DiAngelo recalled in a documentary. "It was a lot of anxiety, trying to keep the camera from shaking, dealing with emotions. Here were people that I loved that were now gone."

After he finished documenting the scene, DiAngelo placed that then-anonymous 911 call to San Diego law enforcement. Rancho Santa Fe would never be the same.

AFTER THE 39 LEFT

The following week, a 58-year-old recluse named Robert Leon Nichols killed himself in his rural home in the foothills of the Sierra Nevada mountains. A *Los Angeles Times* article reported that Nichols, a former Grateful Dead roadie who wrote a book about traveling to Egypt with the band, tied a plastic bag around his head and turned on the propane gas hose in his trailer. He left behind a note that said he was joining the spaceship behind the Hale-Bopp comet. He had covered his body with a purple scarf. Investigators also found a homemade tinfoil spaceship and solar system hanging above Nichols' bed.

The following month, residents of Colina Norte decided to rename their street "Paseo Victoria" after a child who lived on the private street, not to honor the girl but to take the heat off of their now-notorious neighborhood. "We've had weird people stop and get out of their cars and start praying," Rancho Santa Fe resident Diane Doroski told the Associated Press. Neighbors who lived in the "Beverly Hills of San Diego" would later buy the severely devalued mansion for $688,000 (the land itself was valued at $1.5 million) and bulldoze the final resting place of the 39 Heaven's Gate members.

In May 1997, two months after the 39 dead members of Heaven's Gate were discovered, CNN and *60 Minutes* received eerily similar goodbye tapes that pointed them to a Holiday Inn Express in Encinitas, about four miles from the Rancho Santa Fe mansion. Inside room 222 they found the body of Wayne Cook, 45. Charles Humphreys, a computer expert who was the same age, was clinging to life. Both wore black Nikes and were—you guessed it—covered in purple shrouds. Cook, a former playwright and sculptor who had been fascinated with the stars since growing up on a farm in Oklahoma, had lost his wife in the mass suicide. Humphreys was in critical condition, but later released from the hospital (the following year, he would successfully kill himself in the Arizona desert).

Because many of the cult members did not leave behind wills, executing their estates fell on San Diego County. Leading up to a public auction to pay for funeral expenses, two former Heaven's Gate members, Mark and Sarah King, filed a lawsuit and were eventually awarded Applewhite's religious writing and the group's intellectual property, which included the so-called "exit tapes," alien drawings, and T-shirts reading "FARFROMHOME."

In 1999, an auction held at a county government warehouse netted $32,707 in proceeds for the victims' families. Resellers scooped up the infamous bunk beds for a few hundred bucks, and the cult's book collection, which included the *Star Trek Encyclopedia*, *Disneyland of the Gods*, and *Aliens from Outer Space*, for $340. The minivan and moving vans that whisked Heaven's

Gate around were sold off, as well as everyday items that included office chairs, dishes, VCRs, and a small trampoline.

The Los Angeles Museum of Death acquired some items as well, including bunk beds, the black clothes, and purple shrouds that are on display at the Hollywood location, along with a cult recruiting video.

And heavensgate.com, with the red alerts that tipped off authorities to this wild UFO religion, is still active. In March 2017, a *Daily Mail* reporter interviewed the two nameless webmasters who keep the site up and running and claim to be "connected to the Next Level" and still share the group's beliefs. They field about 10 to 12 emails a day, sell a handful of books, and mail about 40 VHS tapes on Heaven's Gate teachings a year. Many speculate that the webmasters are the Phoenix couple who sued for Heaven's Gate's intellectual property in the late nineties.

Nike discontinued the Air model sneakers after the suicides, but collectors can still bid on them on eBay (white Nike Airs could set you back a few hundred dollars, and the iconic black pairs are listed for thousands of dollars). And, with a quick Google search and $8, you too can own a pin replica of the "Heaven's Gate Away Team" patch.

CHAPTER 10

SILVIA MERAZ MORENO'S SANTA MUERTE CULT

She wears a long flowing pink or white wedding gown, a nun's habit, or blue and yellow starred cape, similar to the Virgin of Guadalupe. Though her followers might call her the Woman in White, this is no mother of God, but Santa Muerte, Saint Death.

This Mexican folk saint is beloved by those living in both the light and shadows of society, with devotees ranging from drug traffickers looking for protection to job seekers asking for her help in finding work. She is depicted as having the face of a skeleton, her thin body covered up except for her bony fingers that grip a scythe—the Grim Reapress.

Santa Muerte worship, which has its roots in Mexico's colonial era, was virtually unheard of a generation ago. The cult "came out of the closet," according to religious scholar and Santa Muerte expert Andrew Chesnut, when Enriqueta Romero, known as Doña Queta, put a life-sized statue of Saint Death outside her home in the Mexico City barrio of Tepito on Halloween 2001. The religious offshoot has grown to an estimated 12 million followers since then, according to the *National Post*, with devotees in the United States, United Kingdom, and other countries beyond Mexico. Santa Muerte is considered the fastest-growing new religious movement of our time.

Unlike a canonized saint, which goes through a formal recognition process by the Catholic Church, Santa Muerte is among the dead spirits that are considered holy for their miracle-working powers. She's more approachable, less uptight than a traditional saint—someone you might feel more comfortable turning to for luck in nefarious business dealings than God, the Virgin Mary, or St. Francis of Assisi. She has a number of nicknames, and her followers fondly refer to her as the Pretty Girl, La Flaquita ("skinny girl"), and the Bony Lady.

Earlier in the twentieth century, women might have prayed to Santa Muerte to make her cheating husband faithful again. In recent years, with the ongoing drug war in northern Mexico that has killed thousands of people, Santa Muerte has gained popularity among gangs and prisoners, who look to her for protection. Prayer cards showing Saint Death have also been found on murdered bodies and on the dashboards of cars transporting drugs.

Saint Death has also become a favorite among the poor and other marginalized groups in society, such as transgender women, who might be excluded from attending church or receiving communion and other sacraments. She's been called the "ultimate multitasker," and her followers use different color candles for different kinds of prayers (red for love, gold for money, black for vengeance).

Santa Muerte isn't officially recognized by the Catholic Church. In *National Geographic News*, a Vatican leader denounced the veneration of Saint Death in 2013 as blasphemy "dressed up like religion," and a Vatican-trained exorcist Rezac reported that praying to the Skinny Girl might lead to demonic issues.

In an attempt to discourage Santa Muerte worship, the church suggested St. Jude—the patron saint of hope and lost causes—as an alternative, bumping up his feast day from once a year to once a month. The Mexican government has also played a role in discouraging followers of the Skinny Lady, shutting down a Mexico City Santa Muerte church in 2005 and destroying nearly 40 roadside shrines near the border of California and Texas in 2009. But these warnings haven't stopped Saint Death devotees, who pray to her at these shrines or at their personal home altars, bringing her alcohol, cigarettes, incense, food, and other offerings in exchange for help, wealth, protection, and whatever else they ask for.

It was at one of these home shrines that Silvia Meraz Moreno, 44 at the time of her arrest in 2012, offered more to Holy Death—fresh human blood harvested just for the occasion, with hopes that her holy queen would bring the Morenos desperately needed money.

Moreno lived with her extended family on the outskirts of Nacozari de Garcia in Mexico, a small mining town of about

11,500 people less than 100 miles south of the United States border. Even though Nacozari had largely been spared from the drug cartel violence sweeping northern Mexico, Moreno's family had plenty of other things to worry about. They lived in crude shacks that, by some accounts, had bare dirt floors. The men of the family earned meager incomes by picking through garbage, and a revolving door of unfamiliar men led authorities to believe that the women were working as prostitutes, though authorities could never find enough evidence to make any charges stick. A local church took pity on this down-and-out bunch, giving them used clothes, food, and livestock to help them scrape by.

On three separate occasions from 2009 to 2012, Moreno convinced members of her family to kill three people and offer their blood to the Bony Lady. Illuminated by candlelight, their victims' veins were sliced open while their hearts were still beating. They bled out in this horrifying manner; their blood, pooled and collected in a container, was later given as an offering to Santa Muerte at the family shrine. Investigators reported finding blood evidence spread across more than 30 square meters on the property, and determined that axes and knives were used to carry out the bloody sacrifices. To make a horrifying scene even more grim, two of the victims were 10-year-old boys and allegedly related to the Morenos.

The killings started in 2009 with Moreno's close friend, Cleotilde Romero, 55. In July 2010, the first of the young boys, Martin Rios Chaparro, went missing, and foul play was not suspected because the authorities were told that he had been spotted begging in a nearby town. It wasn't until another

10-year-old boy, Jesus Martinez, went missing in March 2012 that the connection was made between the missing boys and the Moreno family. Silvia Meraz Moreno, then 44, and seven additional family members were arrested the following month. Everyone pointed to Silvia as the ringleader.

Much remains a mystery about Silvia Meraz Moreno and her family cult, described as a Satanic sect by the Sonora State Investigative Police, and this murderous group is certainly the most elusive of this book. What little is known comes from a press conference following the arrest, where Moreno and her family members were lined up, their arms linked, flanked by masked police officers wielding assault-style long guns.

"She was going to offer us money," Moreno told the reporters, referring to Santa Muerte. During the appearance, Moreno clutched a large framed image of Saint Death wearing a red cape and told reporters that she had been devoted to the deity for about two years. Moreno didn't say anything about killing the two boys but confessed that her family killed her friend, Cleotilde Romero, because she was "a witch or something." Most media accounts say the bodies were buried outside of town, but some accounts suggest at least one of the bodies was buried under a child's bedroom floor. The Mexican newspaper *El Mundo* reported that three children aged 1, 2, and 5 witnessed the final human sacrifice and beheading of 10-year-old Jesus Martinez.

Mexican authorities said the Nacozari killings were the first human sacrifice to Saint Death in Sonora that they knew of, but that the killings conjured up the infamous "narco-satanico" killings of the 1980s when 15 bodies, including a missing American college student from Texas on spring break, were found at a ranch outside of Matamoros, Texas. In addition to 75 pounds of marijuana, rotting corpses, missing hearts, eyes, testicles, and other organs were found. Some of the victims were boiled in an oil drum found at the scene, which was covered with human hair, liquor, machetes, and tape. Cult members later testified that the gang believed that the ritual killings would protect them from the police and make them invincible from bullets.

Moreno and her family dropped out of the news after their horrifying arrest, and Moreno is reportedly spending the rest of her life in prison for her ritual acts.

CONCLUSION

At this point, you've likely noticed that cult leaders often have personality traits in common that can range from charming and charismatic to totally terrifying. Perhaps they believe that they're Jesus Christ, the Buddha, or have knowledge to interpret the Bible or other core religious texts that no one in the modern era has. The end of the world is coming, and they know the exact date. Or, they might know how to transcend the average level of human consciousness, and how you can, too. They provide a spiritual answer that their followers have been craving, and might share it, if you leave behind your family, turn over your assets to the group, and drop all shreds of individuality to become part of a collective cause.

And you've learned that cult members are more likely to be idealistic and perhaps vulnerable, not stupid, and have spent their lives searching for spiritual meaning. In a cult, they've perhaps found the answers (at least in the beginning) and been attracted by a cult leader's promise of another way of being and understanding the world.

In countries such as the United States and Japan, religious freedom laws often protect a cult until it can be proven that they've strayed into criminality. US authorities couldn't do much when Jim Jones and his followers emigrated to Guyana, and cults such as Heaven's Gate existed in secrecy. And after the militarized response against the Branch Davidians, the ATF and federal government were often criticized for persecuting a small religious community that kept to themselves in rural Texas. After the Tokyo underground sarin gas attacks in 1995, Japanese authorities could do little more than closely monitor an Aum Shinrikyo splinter group called Aleph, even though it was widely believed that Shoko Asahara continued to lead the group from prison.

In the case of Roch Thériault, Canadian authorities were well aware of "Moses" and his many wives living in the woods. But because cult members refused to betray Thériault, authorities weren't able to intervene until Thériault's wife Gisèle escaped and told authorities about Gabrielle Lavallée's amputation and Boilard's gruesome death and dismembering. After the Solar Temple immolations in a forest outside of Grenoble, French lawmakers successfully introduced legislation to closely monitor cult activity (a move that continues to be condemned by proponents of freedom of expression, as well as the Catholic Church).

Cults might look different from the stereotypical counter-culture groups of the 1960s and 1970s, and today cults are more likely to recruit middle-aged people with money than college students who are less established financially. Cults have embraced the proliferation of self-help groups in popular culture, and might provide training courses as a way to recruit members into their organization.

These groups continue to collectively fascinate us, dominating news headlines and their stories being turned into docuseries. Is it their bizarre worldview or theological interpretations? Or our lurid curiosity regarding the details of their crimes? Or maybe it's our defiance of the idea we could never be convinced to join a cult, or find anything appealing in their message.

Even though we understand a lot about cult leaders and psychology, Dr. Janja Lalich's biggest concern is the stigma and misunderstanding of former cult members, especially the children who have been born into cults.

"There's no resources. There's no shelters. There are few therapists who understand," Lalich said. "I think that society as a whole still holds that stigma, in part, because they can say 'that would never happen to me. I'm too smart.'"

SELECT BIBLIOGRAPHY

ABC News Staff. "Child Survivors Recall Waco Fire 10 Years On." April 17, 2003. https://abcnews.go.com/Primetime/story?id=131981&page=1.

A&E Networks. *Waco, Madman or Messiah*. Directed by Christopher Spencer. Aired January 28 and 29 on A&E Networks. https://www.aetv.com/shows/waco-madman-or-messiah.

Associated Press. "Mexican Border Family Suspected of Human Sacrifice." *NBC News*, April 1, 2012. http://www.nbcnews.com/id/46919631/ns/world_news-americas/t/mexican-border-family-suspected-human-sacrifice/#.WrqLuIhubIU.

Associated Press. "National News Briefs; Vampire Cult Leader Pleads Guilty to Killing 2." February 6, 1998. https://www.nytimes.com/1998/02/06/us/national-news-briefs-vampire-cult-leader-pleads-guilty-to-killing-2.html.

Atchison, Andrew J. and Kathleen M. Heide. "The Application of Sociological Theories to Multiple Murder." *International Journal of Offender Therapy and Comparative Criminology* 55, no. 5 (2010): 780. https://doi.org/10.1177/0306624X10371794.

Barber, Paul. *Vampires, Burial, and Death: Folklore and Reality*. New Haven and London: Yale University Press, 1988.

BBC News Staff. "Kim Jong-nam: VX Dose Was 'High and Lethal.'" *BBC News*. February 26, 2017. https://www.bbc.com/news/world-asia-39096172.

Bearak, Barry. "Eyes on Glory: Pied Pipers of Heaven's Gate." *New York Times*. April 28, 1997. https://www.nytimes.com/1997/04/28/us/eyes-on-glory-pied-pipers-of-heaven-s-gate.html.

Becker, Stephanie. "Judge Decides Grandson Will Get Charles Manson's Body." CNN. March 13, 2018. https://www.cnn.com/2018/03/12/us/charles-manson-body-decision/index.html.

Bell, Michael E. *Food for the Dead: On the Trail of New England's Vampires*. Middletown, Connecticut: Wesleyan University Press, 2001.

Biography.com Editors. "Charles Manson Biography." A&E Television Networks. May 14, 2018. https://www.biography.com/people/charles-manson-9397912.

Bremner, Charles. "Mass Suicide Fears As French Worry That It's Apocalypse, Now." *Times* (London). June 16, 2011. https://infoweb-newsbank-com.proxy.library.nyu.edu/apps/news/document-view?p=AWNB&docref=news/137E8C5FB71D6FA0.

Broad, William. "Sowing Death: A Special Report, How Japan Germ Terror-Alerted the World." *New York Times*. May 26, 1998. https://www.nytimes.com/1998/05/26/world/sowing-death-a-special-report-how-japan-germ-terror-alerted-world.html.

Cahill, Tim. "In the Valley of the Shadow of Death: Guyana After the Jonestown Massacre." *Rolling Stone*. January 25, 1979. https://www.rollingstone.com/culture/news/

in-the-valley-of-the-shadow-of-death-guyana-after-the-jonestown-massacre-19790125.

Campbell, Ramsey. "Vampire Cult Easier To Try Without Heather." *Orlando Sentinel*. December 17, 1997. http://articles.orlandosentinel.com/1997-12-17/news/9712170164_1_ferrell-vampire-cult-cult-member.

Canadian Press. "Solar Temple Children Won't Be Charged." *Kingston Whig-Standard* (Ontario, Canada). April 25, 1997 *NewsBank*. https://infoweb-newsbank-com.proxy.library.nyu.edu/apps/news/document-view?p=AWNB&docref=news/14F44627514B2790.

CBC Digital Archives. "Solar Temple, A Cult Gone Wrong." Last accessed October 9, 2018. https://www.cbc.ca/archives/topic/solar-temple-a-cult-gone-wrong.

Chachere, Vickie, of the Associated Press. "The Signs of Sickness." *Ocala Star Banner*. February 29, 2004. http://www.ocala.com/news/20040229/the-signs-of-sickness.

Chesnut, Andrew. *Devoted to Death: Santa Muerte, the Skeleton Saint*. New York: Oxford University Press, 2018. Google Books edition.

Chryssides, George. *Heaven's Gate: Postmodernity and Pop Culture in a Suicide Group*. Routledge: Oxon, 2016. Google Books edition.

Cole, Benjamin. *The Changing Face of Terrorism: How Real Is the Threat from Biological, Chemical, and Nuclear Weapons?* New York: I.B. Tauris, 2018. Google Books edition.

Collins, Glenn. "The Psychology of the Cult Experience." *New York Times*. March 15, 1982. https://www.nytimes.com/1982/03/15/style/the-psychology-of-the-cult-experience.html.

Dellert, Christine. "Was Cleared in Her Parents' 1996 Murder in Eustis. Now Married and Living Out of State, She Reflects on a Tragic Time." *Orlando Sentinel*. December 17, 2006. http://articles.orlandosentinel.com/2006-12-17/news/WENDORF17_1_ferrell-vampire-eustis-high/2.

Downie Jr., Leonard. "370 More Bodies Discovered in Jonestown." *Washington Post*. November 25, 1978. https://www.washingtonpost.com/archive/politics/1978/11/25/370-more-bodies-discovered-in-jonestown/13d8632e-2d8d-41cc-9c03-7141c1c310bf/?utm_term=.7936529edfc4.

Eggertsen, Chris. "The Manson Murder House." *Curbed Los Angeles*. June 6, 2018. https://la.curbed.com/2018/6/6/17153870/manson-sharon-tate-murder-house-cielo-drive.

Elsass, Peter. *The Psychology of Cultural Resilience in Ethnic Minorities*. New York and London: New York University Press, 1995.

England, Mark. "Decimated Compound Draws Crowds Anyway: 'This Is Going to Be Like Graceland' Shirt Merchant Says." *Waco Tribune Herald*. July 6, 1993. http://www.wacotrib.com/news/branch_davidians/decimated-compound-draws-crowds-anyway-this-is-going-to-be/article_9ee432f9-a089-5507-8765-11cb609d7abe.html.

England, Mark. "What Does Every Prophet Want?—Bible Scholars Promise to Give Howell's Seven Seals Message a Fair Hearing." *Waco Tribune-Herald*. April 15, 1993. http://www.wacotrib.com/news/branch_davidians/what-does-every-prophet-want-bible-scholars-promise-to-give/article_c88aa41d-823f-58cf-9354-913cc8afaf6f.html.

Fagan, Kevin. "Psych Sleuth: Margaret Singer Has Made History Delving Into the Psychology of Brainwashing." *SFGate*. May

26, 2002. https://www.sfgate.com/bayarea/article/PSYCH-SLEUTH-Margaret-Singer-has-made-history-3306807.php.

Federal Bureau of Investigation. "Waco FBI Transcripts Tapes." Last accessed September 15, 2018. https://vault.fbi.gov/waco-branch-davidian-compound.

Folk, Holly. Review of *The Order of the Solar Temple: The Temple of Death*, edited by James R. Lewis. *Communal Societies* 28, no. 2 (2008): 96-98.

Gallagher, Nora. "Jonestown: The Survivors' Story." *New York Times*. November 18, 1979. https://www.nytimes.com/1979/11/18/archives/jonestown-the-survivors-story-jonestown.html.

Gladwell, Malcolm. "Sacred and Profane: How Not to Negotiate With Believers." *New Yorker*. March 31, 2014. https://www.newyorker.com/magazine/2014/03/31/sacred-and-profane-4.

Guillermoprieto, Alma. "Vatican in a Bind About Santa Muerte." *National Geographic News*. May 4, 2013. https://news.nationalgeographic.com/news/2013/13/130512-vatican-santa-muerte-mexico-cult-catholic-church-cultures-world.

Guinn, Jeff. *The Life and Times of Charles Manson*. New York: Simon and Schuster, 2013.

Hadden, Gerry. "The French Want To Make Society Safe for Religion by Banning So-Called Cults." Public Radio International. July 12, 2014. Accessed August 28, 2018. https://www.pri.org/stories/2014-07-12/french-want-make-society-safe-religion-banning-so-called-cults.

Haldeman, Bonnie and Catherine Wessinger, *Memories of the Branch Davidians: The Autobiography of David Koresh's Mother*. Waco, TX: Baylor University Press, 2007.

Hamilton, Matt and Shelby Grad. "Manson Follower's Chilling Murder Description: 'We Started Stabbing and Cutting Up the Lady.'" *Los Angeles Times.* April 15, 2016. http://www.latimes.com/local/lanow/la-me-ln-manson-followers-chilling-description-20160415-story.html#.

Hamm, Mark S. "Apocalyptic Violence: The Seduction of Terrorist Subcultures." *Theoretical Criminology* 8, no. 3 (2004): 323-339. https://doi.org/10.1177%2F1362480604044612.

Hart, Lianne. "Puny Market for Davidian Muscle Car—David Koresh's Pride and Joy Fails to Excite Many Bidders." *Los Angeles Times.* September 26, 2004. https://www.sfgate.com/news/article/Puny-market-for-Davidian-muscle-car-David-2691411.php.

Hernon, Matthew. "20 Years After the Aum Shinrikyo Attacks, A Former Leader Speaks Out." *Tokyo Weekender.* March 13, 2015. https://www.tokyoweekender.com/2015/03/20-years-after-the-aum-shinrikyo-attacks-a-former-leader-speaks-out.

Hewitt, Bill, Thoman Fields-Meyer, Bruce Frankel, Dan Jewell, Pam Lambert, Anne-Marie O'Neill, and William Plummer. "Who They Were." *People.* April 14, 1997. http://people.com/archive/cover-story-who-they-were-vol-47-no-14.

Hirsley, Michael. "Adventists Kicked Out Cult, Leader." *Chicago Tribune.* March 2, 1993. http://articles.chicagotribune.com/1993-03-02/news/9303186458_1_davidians-george-roden-marc-breault.

Jacobs, David. *Blood and Lust.* New York: Pinnacle Books, 2000.

Japan Times Staff. "Aleph Raided Over Alleged Lease Fraud." February 19, 2018. https://www.japantimes.co.jp/news/

2018/02/19/national/crime-legal/aleph-raided-alleged-lease-fraud/#.WyJXx6czbIU.

Jeffreys, Daniel. "Blood Ties." *Independent*. December 5, 1996. https://www.independent.co.uk/life-style/blood-ties-1313032.html.

Jiji. "Death Row Inmate and Former Aum Shinrikyo Member Publishes VX Research Paper." *Japan Times*. May 24, 2018. https://www.japantimes.co.jp/?post_type=news&p=1416366#.Wx56VvZuLIU.

Jones, Aphrodite. *The Embrace: A True Vampire Story*. New York: Pocket Books, 1999.

Jordan, Mary and Sue Anne Pressley. "Gruesome Contest to Raise Dead Led to Koresh's Takeover of Cult." *Washington Post*. March 7, 1993. https://www.washingtonpost.com/archive/politics/1993/03/07/gruesome-contest-to-raise-dead-led-to-koreshs-takeover-of-cult/3696fc28-cc9f-4f50-9d83-5dec6593e06c/?utm_term=.b487887a8dff.

Kaihla, Paul and Ross Laver. *Savage Messiah*. Toronto: Doubleday Canada Limited, 1993.

Kaplan, David E. and Andrew Marshall. "The Cult at the End of the World." *Wired*. July 1, 1996. https://www.wired.com/1996/07/aum.

Kerstetter, Todd. "'That's Just the American Way': The Branch Davidian Tragedy and Western Religious History." *The Western Historical Quarterly* 35, no. 4 (2004): 455, accessed July 2, 2018. https://www.jstor.org/stable/25443054.

Kilduff, Marshall and Phil Tracy. "Inside Peoples Temple." *New West*. August 1, 1977. https://jonestown.sdsu.edu/wp-content/uploads/2013/10/newWestart.pdf.

Klarenberg, Kit. "Exclusive: Meet the Man Battling Dangerous Cults Wherever He Finds Them." *Sputnik News*. March 3, 2018. https://sputniknews.com/analysis/201803121062378148-ukcults-danger-group

Kramer, Michael J. "Summer of Love, Summer of War." *New York Times*. August 15, 2017. https://www.nytimes.com/2017/08/15/opinion/vietnam-san-francisco-1967-summer.html.

Lacayo, Richard. "In the Reign of Fire." *Time*. June 24, 2001. http://content.time.com/time/magazine/article/0,9171,163068,00.html.

Langlois, Jill. "Santa Muerte Cult Kills 3 as Human Sacrifices in Mexico." *PRI*. March 31, 2012. https://www.pri.org/stories/2012-03-31/santa-muerte-cult-kills-3-human-sacrifices-mexico.

Lewis, James R., ed. *The Order of the Solar Temple: The Temple of Death*. Abingdon and New York: Routledge, 2016.

Lindsey, Robert. "Jim Jones—From Poverty to Power of Life and Death." *New York Times*. November 26, 1978. https://www.nytimes.com/1978/11/26/archives/jim-jonesfrom-poverty-to-power-of-life-and-death-arrested-for-lewd.html.

Lifton, Robert Jay. *Destroying the World to Save It: Aum Shinrikyo, Apocalyptic Violence, and the New Global Terrorism*. New York: Henry Holt and Company, 1999, Google Books edition.

Lifton, Robert Jay. "In the Lord's Hands: America's Apocalyptic Mindset." *World Policy Journal* 20, no. 3 (2003): 62. *JSTOR Journals*, EBSCO*host* (accessed August 27, 2018).

Lipka, Michael. "The Most and Least Racially Diverse U.S. Religious Groups." Pew Research Center. July 27, 2015. Accessed July 04, 2018. http://www.pewresearch.org/

fact-tank/2015/07/27/the-most-and-least-racially-diverse-u-s-religious-groups.

Long, William R. "Little Remains of Peoples Temple Outpost Where 913 Died: 10 Years Later, Jonestown is a Site of Silent Desolation." *Los Angeles Times.* November 18, 1988. http://articles.latimes.com/1988-11-18/news/mn-468_1_peoples-temple.

Manson, Charles and Nuel Emmons. *Manson in His Own Words: The Shocking Confessions of "The Most Dangerous Man Alive."* New York: Grove Press, 1986. Google Books edition.

Mayer, Jean Francois. "The Case of the Solar Temple" and "Comments on the 'Pathology of Charismatic Leadership'" (presentation, Apocalyptic Millennialism in the West: The Case of the Solar Temple, Charlottesville, VA, November 13, 1998). https://med.virginia.edu/ciag/wp-content/uploads/sites/313/2015/12/report_apocalyptic_millennialism_c1998.pdf.

McCormick, Darlene. "Mount Carmel 'Requiem' Lures About 75 Listeners." *Waco Tribune-Herald.* October 24, 1993. http://www.wacotrib.com/news/branch_davidians/mount-carmel-requiem-lures-about-listeners/article_1c41d65a-0a36-5477-83cc-614dfb849725.html.

McCormick, Darlene and Mark England. "Sinful Messiah: The Law Watches, But Has Done Little." *Waco Tribune-Herald.* February 27, 1993. https://www.wacotrib.com/news/branch_davidians/sinful-messiah/the-sinful-messiah-the-law-watches-but-has-done-little/article_fb999940-0b23-5b11-95ea-3a6f0c9b1f06.html.

McKay, Rich. "Sheriff Hopes Wendorf Will Be Tried in Parents' Slayings." *Orlando Sentinel.* December 12,

1998. http://articles.orlandosentinel.com/1998-12-12/
news/9812120058_1_wendorf-grand-jury-knupp.

McKie, Robin. "Charles Manson Follower Ends Her Silence 40
Years After Night of Slaughter." *Guardian*. August 2, 2009.
https://www.theguardian.com/world/2009/aug/02/charles-
manson-linda-kasabian-polanski.

Meadows, Karin. "Keesee Drinks Blood In Prison." *Orlando
Sentinel*. December 11, 1998. http://articles.orlandosentinel
.com/1998-12-11/news/9812100770_1_wendorf-currington-
keesee.

Meier, Barry. "Inside a Secretive Group Where Women Are
Branded." *New York Times*. October 17, 2017. https://www.ny
times.com/2017/10/17/nyregion/nxivm-women-branded-
albany.html.

Metraux, Daniel A. "Religious Terrorism in Japan: The Fatal
Appeal of Aum Shinrikyo." *Asian Survey* 35, no. 12 (1995):
1140-154. doi:10.2307/2645835.

Montreal Gazette Staff. "Leader, 3 Cult Members Responsible in
Tot's Death." December 18, 1981. https://news.google.com/
newspapers?nid=1946&dat=19811218&id=eSsiAAAAIBAJ
&sjid=KaUFAAAAIBAJ&pg=4623,4261740.

Murphy, Mary. "Inmate: Cultist Blames Ferrell." *Orlando
Sentinel*. January 4, 1997. http://articles.orlandosentinel
.com/1997-01-04/news/9701031513_1_ferrell-scott-
anderson-wendorf.

Nelson, Stanley, *Jonestown: The Life and Death of Peoples Temple*,
(2006; Firelight Media Inc., American Experience, New York),
documentary video.

Nossiter, Adam. "Warning of Violence Was Unheeded After
Cult Leader's Gun Battle in '87." *New York Times*. March

10, 1993. https://www.nytimes.com/1993/03/10/us/
warning-of-violence-was-unheeded-after-cult-leader-s-
gun-battle-in-87.html.

Onishi, Norimitsu. "After 8-Year Trial in Japan, Cultist Is
Sentenced to Death." *New York Times.* February 28, 2004.
https://www.nytimes.com/2004/02/28/world/after-
8-year-trial-in-japan-cultist-is-sentenced-to-death.
html?pagewanted=all.

Oprah.com. "Jim Jones Jr. Speaks Out." February 17, 2010. http://
www.oprah.com/oprahshow/mass-murderer-jim-jones-
son-speaks-out/all#ixzz58Jb6Ioq9.

Palmer, Susan J. "War on Sects: A Post 9/11 Update." *Nova Religio*
11, no. 3 (2009): 104-120. *Jstor* (accessed August 27, 2018).

Parachini, John. "Aum Shinrikyo." In *Aptitude for Destruction,
Volume 2: Case Studies of Organizational Learning in Five
Terrorist Groups*, 11-36. Santa Monica, CA; Arlington, VA;
Pittsburgh, PA: RAND Corporation, 2005.

Pearson, Muriel, Wilking, Spencer, and Effron, Lauren.
"Survivors of 1993 Waco Siege Describe Fire That Ended
the 51-Day Standoff." *ABC News.* January 30, 2018. https://
abcnews.go.com/US/survivors-1993-waco-siege-describe-
happened-fire-ended/story?id=52034435.

Perry, Tony. "Cult Members Enjoyed Many Earthly Pleasures."
Los Angeles Times. April 3, 1997. http://articles.latimes.com/
1997-04-03/news/mn-44907_1_cult-members.

Pitts, William L. "Davidians and the Branch Davidians." Hand-
book of Texas Online, June 12, 2010, accessed July 02, 2018.
http://www.tshaonline.org/handbook/online/articles/
ird01.

Pollack, Andrew. "Japanese Police Find Body of a Lawyer Believed to Be Killed by Cult." *New York Times.* September 7, 1995. https://www.nytimes.com/1995/09/07/world/japanese-police-find-body-of-a-lawyer-believed-killed-by-cult.html.

QMI Agency. "Killed Cult Leader's Sons Speak Out." *Whig.* March 13, 2011. http://www.thewhig.com/2011/03/13/killed-cult-leaders-sons-speak-out.

Rainey, James "The Cult in Hindsight: Diamond Bar Woman Recalls Group's Beginning and the Unease That Turned Into a Crusade Against It." *Los Angeles Times.* March 30, 1997. http://articles.latimes.com/1997-03-30/news/mn-43687_1_diamond-bar.

Reid, T.R. "The Doomsayer Guru." *Washington Post.* March 24, 1995. https://www.washingtonpost.com/archive/politics/1995/03/24/the-doomsayer-guru/8954878b-c05f-4c7b-ba88-189a3750ed11/?noredirect=on&utm_term=.792eeb7327a8.

Richardson, James T. Massimo Introvigne. "'Brainwashing' Theories in European Parliamentary and Administrative Reports on 'Cults' and 'Sects.'" *Journal for the Scientific Study of Religion* 40, no. 2 (2001): 143. http://www.jstor.org/stable/1387941.

Sanders, Ed. *The Family: The Story of Charles Manson's Dune Buggy Attack.* New York: E.P. Dutton and Co., Inc, 1971, 94.

Bugliosi, Vincent and Curt Gentry. *Helter Skelter.* New York: W.W. Norton & Company, 1974.

Sarr, Matthew. "Manson Funeral Held in Porterville." *Porterville Recorder* (California). March 19, 2018. http://www.recorderonline.com/news/manson-funeral-held-in-

porterville/article_e69805a8-2bd1-11e8-9c72-1fb904b061a2
.html.

Singer, Margaret Thaler and Janja Lalich. *Cults in our Midst: The Hidden Menace in Our Everyday Lives*. San Francisco: Jossey-Bass Publishers, 1995.

Smith, J.B. "20 Years Later, No Public Memorials, Ceremonies Mark Mount Carmel Saga." *Waco Herald Tribune*. February 28, 2013. http://www.wacotrib.com/news/mclennan_county/years-later-no-public-memorials-ceremonies-mark-mount-carmel-saga/article_d5ed44bb-51dd-5f81-80f0-f6a8a2357979.html.

Soares, John. "Trying to Wear the White Hat: Nixon, the Media, and the Chisum-Charles Manson Imbroglio." *Western Historical Quarterly* 46, no. 4 (2015): 448-449.

Stanfield, Frank. "Ferrell's Mind Impaired." *Orlando Sentinel*. February 18, 1998. http://articles.orlandosentinel.com/1998-02-18/news/9802180358_1_ferrell-krop-vampire.

Stanfield, Frank and Lesley Clark. "'I Want Them Alive,' Heather Warned Cultist." *Orlando Sentinel*. February 5, 1997. http://articles.orlandosentinel.com/1997-02-05/news/9702041312_1_ferrell-heather-wendorf.

Stanfield, Frank. "Mom Paints Softer Portrait of Her Son." *Orlando Sentinel*. January 21, 1998. http://articles.orlandosentinel.com/1998-01-21/news/9801210301_1_ferrell-wendorf-gibson.

Stanfield, Frank. "Mother, Son Caught In Cult's Web." *Orlando Sentinel*. February 6, 1997. http://articles.orlandosentinel.com/1997-02-06/news/9702051380_1_ferrell-vampire-gibson.

Stanfield, Frank. "'Rod Is A Good Boy,' Grandparents Say." *Orlando Sentinel*. January 11, 1998. http://articles.orlando sentinel.com/1998-01-11/news/9801100795_1_gibson-ferrell-rosetta.

Stanfield, Frank. "Wendorf Family Still Bears Murders' Pain." *Orlando Sentinel*. November 23, 1997. http://articles.orlando sentinel.com/1997-11-23/news/9711220474_1_wendorf-ruth-friends-and-family.

Steinberg, Jacques. "From Religious Childhood to Reins of a U.F.O. Cult." *New York Times*. March 29, 1997. https://www.nytimes.com/1997/03/29/us/from-religious-childhood-to-reins-of-a-ufo-cult.html.

Steinke, Darcey. "God Rocks: Our 1993 Feature on the Siege in Waco, Texas." *Spin*. November 6, 2015. https://www.spin.com/featured/david-koresh-waco-texas-1993-siege-feature.

Thibodeau, David and Leon Whiteson with Aviva Layton. *Waco: A Survivor's Story*. New York: Hachette Books, 2018.

Thomas, Pierre. "Koresh Called '911' When Raid Began." *Washington Post*. June 10, 1993. https://www.washingtonpost.com/archive/politics/1993/06/10/koresh-called-911-when-raid-began/cfa51956-91a8-499b-8b27-bf06228a1eb3/?utm_term=.ae99849ecd65.

"From Mysticism to Murder: Larence Shainberg Interviews Robert Jay Lifton on Aum Shinrikyo." *Tricycle: The Buddhist Review*. Winter 1997. https://tricycle.org/magazine/from-mysticism-to-murder.

Tucker, Abigail. "The Great New England Vampire Panic." *Smithsonian Magazine*. October 2012. https://www.smithsonianmag.com/history/the-great-new-england-vampire-panic-36482878.

Verhovek, Sam Howe. "5 Years After Waco Standoff, The Spirit of Koresh Lingers." *New York Times.* April 19, 1998. https://www.nytimes.com/1998/04/19/us/5-years-after-waco-standoff-the-spirit-of-koresh-lingers.html.

Vevel, Lawrence and R. Lawrence *Cults: An In Depth Look At The Experience Of Being In Cults And Breaking Free From Them*, (Massachusetts School of Law, Andover, Massachusetts) video recording. https://www.youtube.com/watch?v=VJ1w6lgrttE.

Waco Tribune-Herald Staff. "Editorial: Pitiful Display At Courthouse." April 22, 1988. https://www.wacotrib.com/news/branch_davidians/editorial-pitiful-display-at-courthouse/article_0c0f6d90-7afa-55e7-99f5-69eb51d90dd8.html.

Weller, Sheila. "Suddenly That Summer." *Vanity Fair.* July 2012. https://www.vanityfair.com/culture/2012/07/lsd-drugs-summer-of-love-sixties.

White, Megan and Hatim A. Omar. "Vampirism, Vampire Cults and the Teenager of Today." *International Journal of Adolescent Medicine and Health* 22, no. 2 (2010): 190, accessed August 8, 2018. https://uknowledge.uky.edu/pediatrics_facpub/75.

Wilking, Spencer. "ATF Agents At Fatal 1993 Waco Raid Describe Being Under Barrage of Gunfire." *ABC News.* January 5, 2018. https://abcnews.go.com/US/atf-agents-fatal-1993-waco-raid-describe-barrage/story?id=52148324.

Woods, William Crawford. "From the Stacks: 'Demon in the Counterculture." *New Republic.* August 8, 2013. https://newrepublic.com/article/114233/stacks-charles-manson-helter-skelter-and-counterculture.

Wrath, Gary. "'I lost count at 10'—Encinitas deputy recalls day he discovered grisly mass suicide." *San Diego Union-Tribune*. March 26, 2007. http://www.sandiegouniontribune. com/sdut-i-lost-count-at-10-encinitas-deputy-recalls-day-2007mar26-story.html.

Wray, Daniel Dylan. "This Is How Cults Work." *Vice*. December 16, 2014. https://www.vice.com/en_us/article/wd49g9/uk-cult-information-centre-interview-202.

Wright, Stuart A. "Revisiting the Branch Davidian Mass Suicide Debate." *Nova Religio: The Journal of Alternative and Emergent Religions* 12, no. 2 (2009): 4-24. http://www.jstor.org/stable/10.1525/nr.2009.13.2.4?origin=JSTOR-pdf.

Yardley, Jim. "Government Cleared in Deaths at Waco." *New York Times*. September 21, 2000. https://www.nytimes.com/2000/09/21/us/government-cleared-in-deaths-at-waco.html.

Zeller, Benjamin Z. *Heaven's Gate: America's UFO Religion*. New York: New York University Press, 2014. Google Books edition, 65, 70.

ACKNOWLEDGMENTS

Thank you to the team at Ulysses Press, especially Casie Vogel, and my friends, family, and mentors, who have always encouraged, challenged, and believed in me.

ABOUT THE AUTHOR

Wendy Joan Biddlecombe Agsar has worked as a reporter and editor in Florida and New York City. She splits her time between Germany and the United States with her husband, Sam, and their cat, Chicken. This is her first book.